643.7

THE FANTASTIC
HOME MAINTENANCE
MANUAL FEATURING
CAPTAIN COMPETENT
AND THE TOOLBELT OF POWER

THE FANTASTIC
HOME MAINTENANCE
MANUAL FEATURING
CAPTAIN COMPETENT
AND THE TOOLBELT OF POWER

GILL PAUL with MIKE LAWRENCE

Illustrated by IVAN HISSEY

Aurum

First published in Great Britain
in 2006 by
AURUM PRESS LTD
25 Bedford Avenue
London, WC1B 3AT

ISBN 1-84513-158-4
Copyright © The Ivy Press Limited 2006

All do-it-yourself activities involve a degree of risk. Skills, materials, tools and site conditions vary widely.
Although the author and publisher have made every effort to ensure accuracy, the reader remains
responsible for the selection and use of tools, materials and methods. Always follow the manufacturer's
operating instructions and observe safety precautions. Note: the electrical jobs featured in this book are
outside the scope of the new UK electrical safety regulations (Part P of the Building Regulations), which
came into effect in January 2005. You can therefore tackle them without the need to contact your local
authority Building Control department.

THE IVY PRESS LIMITED
The Old Candlemakers
West Street
Lewes, East Sussex BN7 2NZ

Creative Director   PETER BRIDGEWATER
Publisher   SOPHIE COLLINS
Editorial Director   JASON HOOK
Senior Project Editor   CAROLINE EARLE
Designer   CLARE BARBER
Illustrations   IVAN HISSEY
Text   GILL PAUL
Technical Advisor   MIKE LAWRENCE

Printed and bound in China

1 3 5 7 9 10 8 6 4 2 1

CONTENTS

EVEN A SUPERHERO NEEDS DECENT SHELVING! DON THE TOOLBELT OF POWER AND ENTER MY FANTASTIC WORLD OF DIY!

THE TRUE STORY OF CAPTAIN COMPETENT AND KEVIN KLUTZ

DON'T EVEN TRY TO DIY, KEV

Kevin is a nice guy. His mother adores him and so does his gorgeous girlfriend Caroline. You'd like him if you met him — unless, that is, you ever trusted him to do a DIY job in your home. When it comes to practical matters, Kevin is completely cack-handed, but the problem is that he doesn't seem to realize it because he keeps trying to do jobs he's utterly incapable of.

The curtain rail he put up for his mother fell on her head the first time she tried to close the curtains. His shelves slope from side to side and back to front, as Caroline found out when she rested a cup of coffee on one. When he nailed down a loose floorboard in his hall, he hit a water pipe and created a brand-new fountain feature.

That's not all. There's the time when he put a new plug on his kettle and fused the whole house. Or when he painted his bedroom ceiling with a roller and sprayed everything in the room with white paint — including Fluffy the cat. His wallpaper curls off the wall as soon as he turns to paste the next strip. And the tiling in his bathroom slopes so badly that it makes you feel seasick.

A BEDROOM FARCE

You'd think, after a string of disasters like these, that Kevin would cut his losses and accept his incompetence. There are plenty of professionals out there trying to earn a living. Why not hire them instead?

But no! When his twin nieces wanted bunk beds in their bedroom, who volunteered to construct the flatpack? You guessed it. And have they been sleeping peacefully in them ever since? Absolutely not — they wouldn't touch them with a bargepole.

MAYBE THEY INCLUDED EXTRA PIECES IN CASE SOME GOT LOST? ON THE OTHER HAND, THESE DON'T LOOK LIKE ANY BUNK BEDS I'VE EVER SEEN...

Maybe it's because there were several important-looking pieces left over at the end and they didn't accept Kevin's explanation that they must be 'spares'. Perhaps it's just the very wonky angles of the whole unit. I wouldn't get on it – would you?

The longer Kevin lives in his house, the more things get broken or damaged, so he spends more and more of his time trying to fix them. Caroline finds it strangely endearing, but you'll notice that she never asks him to fix anything in her house. Goodness no.

A VERY IMPORTANT LETTER

The situation would probably have deteriorated until the house was uninhabitable, except that one morning Kevin got an official-looking letter in the post. It was from a law firm called Ruthers and Struthers. He read it carefully, then read it again. Seemingly his great-uncle Philip had passed away and Kevin was invited to stop by the lawyers' office to pick up a bequest. Kevin was very surprised by this, since he'd only met great-uncle Philip twice, and the last time he'd offered to hang a picture on the wall for him and drilled into an electric cable, with shocking results. What on earth could Philip have left him? And why?

Money, he hoped. He could do with a new car, or a nice summer holiday, or a good set of golf clubs.

When he was shown into the lawyers' office, though, it wasn't a cheque sitting on the desk. Instead there was a large, worn toolbelt filled with all kinds of home-maintenance tools. Kevin looked around the room to see if there could be some mistake. Where was the money? The paintings? The priceless artefacts? With great solemnity Mr Struthers presented him with the toolbelt.

A STRANGE TRANSFORMATION

Kevin didn't want to appear ungrateful, but whoever heard of such a peculiar bequest? And how could a belt of tools teach him anything he didn't know already? Grumpily he carried it home. He walked down the hall, with its squeaking floorboards, and into the kitchen, flinging the door open violently – whereupon there was a clatter as the much-abused door fell off its hinges. Kevin threw the toolbelt on the table, in a foul mood now, and picked up the kettle to make a cup of coffee – before he remembered that it didn't work any more.

Now, Kevin is not given to cursing but, if he had been, he would have cursed at that very moment. He put a pan of water on the stove and stood waiting for it to boil. The toolbelt lay on the table where he'd thrown it, the edge of a chisel glinting in the morning light. Something compelled Kevin to look more closely. He could see a hammer, screwdrivers, saws – in fact, the toolbelt appeared to hold a miraculous number of tools, yet it hadn't been heavy as he carried it home. Wasn't that strange?

He picked it up and, sure enough, it wasn't heavy at all, despite all the metal tools in its pockets. Then he experienced a strange sensation, a kind of compulsion to put the toolbelt on. He fastened it carefully around his waist – and an extraordinary transformation occurred. Instead of weedy, speccy Kevin, there stood a cartoon superhero, complete with bristling biceps, a stunning six-pack – and red underpants on top of blue lycra leggings.

The superhero spoke: 'I'm Captain Competent, the greatest of the great, the handiest of the handy, the champion DIY superhero of the universe, and my feats are renowned across the solar system and throughout time.... Let's see. Seems as though there's going to be a lot of work to do around here. Look at that door. Tut, tut. What a klutz Kevin must be.'

The Captain pottered around the house, checking out all Kevin's DIY disasters. When he got back to the kitchen, the water was boiling. 'I'll just let the little fella have his coffee before we start. Looks like there's no time to lose.'

The Captain took the toolbelt off again and Kevin reappeared, very shaken. 'Who on earth was that? It felt very bizarre – I was inside a body that wasn't my own, and I felt different. Spookily different. When I ... or we ... looked around at everything that's broken in the house, somehow I knew what had to be done. I knew how to fix them all. What an incredible gift great-uncle Philip has given me, if this is true.'

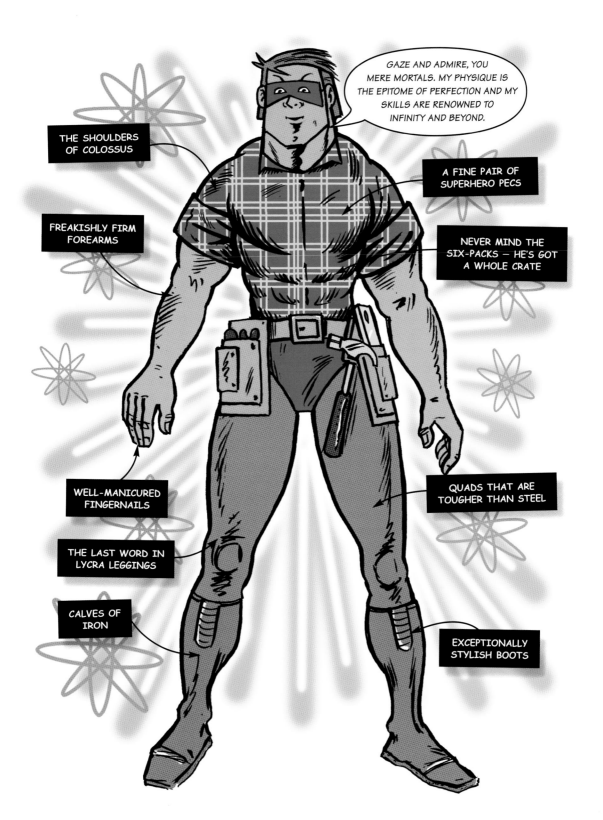

THE CAPTAIN'S BASICS
WHAT'S IN HIS TOOLBELT?

OK, YOU GUYS, READY FOR LESSON ONE? THIS IS A HAMMER AND WE USE IT FOR HAMMERING. GOT THAT? ARE YOU SURE?

GETTING TOOLED UP

Fancy becoming competent yourself? We can't promise instant transformation into a muscled superhero, but you should manage most common household repairs yourself with a few basic tools:

SCREWDRIVERS

You'll need a range of sizes – small, medium and large – with both flat tips and cross tips (for fitting screws with X-shaped indentations on top).

HAMMERS

These come in all sizes and weights, but a good basic one weighs around 340 g (12 oz). A cross-peen hammer has one rounded and one flat head, and it is good for driving in small nails. A claw hammer (like the one the Captain's holding) has a claw on the back of the head for pulling out nails.

NAIL PUNCH

Invaluable for driving the heads of nails below the surface. You'll need to use one of these before you sand a wooden floor, so the nail heads don't rip the sanding paper.

SAWS

A general-purpose hand saw with around 8 teeth per 25 mm (1 in) is a good starting point. The golden rule of saws is the more teeth per inch, the smoother the cut will be. Tenon saws have a stiffened top edge and square ends, and they are used for finer, more accurate cutting. You might need a padsaw, also known as a keyhole saw, which is good for cutting holes in panels.

G-CLAMP

For holding wood or tiles steady while you cut them. Go for a fast-action clamp rather than a traditional one, as it's easier to use.

PLIERS

How else could you pull out little panel pins without a pair of combination pliers? Standard 180 mm (7 in) ones are useful for several gripping and twisting jobs.

CRAFT KNIFE

Also known as a utility knife, this can cut through a range of materials, including carpet and vinyl, and is good for marking cutting lines on wood. Choose one with a retractable blade, and buy several replacement blades.

CHISELS

Woodworking chisels are essential for cutting notches in wood, for example when you're fitting new door locks. They come with bevelled and straight edges. Start with 6 mm (¼ in) and 19 mm (¾ in) bevelled versions (*see page 22 for tips on* keeping them sharp). Don't confuse these with bolster chisels, which are larger, and are used for cutting through brickwork and general levering jobs.

BRADAWL

A useful little gadget for starting holes in wood, or marking drilling positions in plaster.

PLANE

For shaving and smoothing wood that needs to be reduced a little. A bench plane about 250 mm (10 in) long will do for most basic woodworking jobs around the house – but they're tricky for beginners to master (see page 32 for some tips).

SURFORM

An alternative to a plane that is much easier to use, although you'll have to sand the surface afterwards to smooth it. They're like glorified cheese graters with handles on top.

METAL FILE

For rounding off sharp edges. Just like a nail file, but tougher. Obviously.

ADJUSTABLE SPANNERS

These are for gripping nuts of all sizes, to loosen or tighten them. The most useful sizes to have in your toolbox are 255 mm (10¼ in) and 350 mm (14 in) long. You won't be able to undo stiff plumbing fittings without one of these.

SPIRIT LEVEL

You'll need this for most DIY tasks, to check your horizontals are truly horizontal and verticals are vertical. A 900 mm (3 ft) model will do for most indoor work.

TRY SQUARE

For checking right angles, or marking cutting lines at 90° to a surface. Test it from time to time, to make sure the blade hasn't slipped out of alignment. Hold your try square against a piece of wood with a straight edge and draw a line against

the blade, running across the wood. Now turn the try square over and check that the line you've drawn still follows the blade edge. If it doesn't, your try square is out of true.

STRAIGHTEDGE

If you're joining up two cutting points, don't think of doing it without a straightedge. Choose one that's between 1.4 m (4 ft 6 in) and 1.8 m (6 ft) long. You could use any rigid piece of smooth timber, but check that it's completely straight – or use a long steel rule instead.

RETRACTABLE STEEL TAPE MEASURE

Buy a sturdy tape measure. You'll need one that's at least 3 m (10 ft) long.

ABRASIVE PAPER

For sanding wood and plaster; this is easiest to use when wrapped around a sanding block. It comes in coarse, medium and fine grades. The larger the grit specification, the finer the grit, so 400 grit is finer than 200 grit.

PENCILS

Keep one tucked behind your ear for that authentic builder's look, or stick them in your toolbelt. They should be sharp, with hard points, for marking cutting holes and fixing positions, and all kinds of lines, as well as jotting down measurements.

DON'T RELY ON MEMORY WHEN TAKING MEASUREMENTS – WRITE THEM DOWN! FOUR BY SIX IS DIFFERENT FROM SIX BY FOUR. AND IS THAT METRES OR FEET?

I GOT THE POWER
AND YOU SHOULD GET SOME TOO

You won't get far without a decent power drill – hand drills went out with the Ark. Purchase wisely and you'll find there are all kinds of dinky accessories that can make it a neat, multi-purpose DIY buddy.

CHOOSING YOUR DRILL

The first decision you'll have to make is whether you want a cordless drill. These are generally less powerful than mains drills, but they mean you don't need to trail extension leads all over the house to reach the site where you're working. A basic cordless drill will drill fifty 13 mm (½ in) holes in softwood before the battery needs recharging – which, you must admit, is not bad going.

If you want a drill with more power and a wider range of functions, opt for a mains drill. Choose one with variable speed to allow you to drill into different materials. A single-speed drill operating at about 2500 revs a minute would be fine for drilling small holes in wood (up to 10 mm/⅜ in) but if you want bigger holes or to use your drill in masonry, you'll need slower speeds to prevent damage to the drill bit (and the wall).

For drilling into masonry, choose a drill that has hammer action. If you want to use your drill as an electric screwdriver, pick one with a slow-speed, high-torque feature and reverse action so you can undo screws as well.

HOW MUCH POWER WILL YOU NEED?

A basic drill motor is around 400 watts, and this will be suitable for most general household tasks. The state-of-the-art Big-Boy drills have motors of up to 1080 watts, and they can drill into concrete and steel while simultaneously mowing the lawn and preparing a gourmet dinner (joke).

And you'll need to know about chucks. These are the jaws that clasp the drill bit or accessory. The bigger the chuck, the bigger the bit it can take. A chuck of 13 mm (½ in) will be enough for general work, and can take a range of accessories as well. Basic cordless drills only have a chuck of 10 mm (⅜ in). Some cheap drills have chucks that need to be tightened with a key – in this case, ask your DIY store for a spare key in case you lose it – but most now have keyless chucks.

ZROOM ZROOM

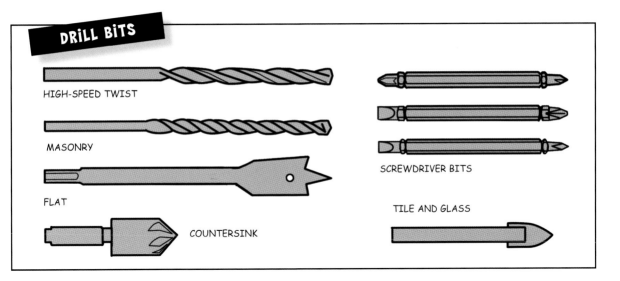

DRILL BITS

HIGH-SPEED TWIST

MASONRY

FLAT

COUNTERSINK

SCREWDRIVER BITS

TILE AND GLASS

CHOOSING YOUR BITS

Some drills come with a complete set of bits, but if yours doesn't, there's no need to buy them all. Here's what the Captain recommends for basic interior DIY tasks:

High-speed twist bits come in sizes from 1 mm to 13 mm (¹⁄₃₂ in to ½ in). Choose 1.8 mm (¹⁄₁₆ in), 2.5 mm (³⁄₃₂ in) and 5 mm (³⁄₁₆ in) bits for drilling pilot and clearance holes to take the most commonly used wood screws (see pages 16 and 26 for more on screwing). You can always buy more bits when you need to use other sizes of screw.

You will also need a countersink drill bit for driving the heads of countersunk screws just below the surface of the wood.

Masonry bits made of hardened tungsten carbide will be needed if you're planning on drilling into masonry walls.

Flat bits are used when you need to make larger holes in wood – more than 13 mm (½ in). They come in sizes from 8 mm (⅜ in) up to around 40 mm (1⅝ in).

Screwdriver bits also come in a range of sizes that you should match to the sizes of the screws. Buy a set and they'll throw in a free box that you can keep them in!

And there are specialist drill bits for working in tricky materials, like tiles and glass. Buy them if or when you need them.

CUTTING AND SANDING

If you've got a lot of wood to cut, a power jigsaw is a good investment – and they're not very expensive. You just have to fit the right blade, switch on and off you go. They can cut curves, if you need to, and there are cordless varieties available. (There's more about sawing on pages 30–1.)

Rotary sanders are circular abrasive drill attachments that are suitable for small sanding jobs – if you're doing a lot of sanding, it's worth buying or hiring a separate power sander (see pages 106–9).

USING YOUR POWER WISELY
* Always unplug the drill before you change an attachment.
* Check occasionally that the chuck has not worked loose due to vibrations.
* Wear appropriate safety gear (see pages 14–15), and ensure that long hair is tied back and no loose clothing can get in the way.
* Never lift a drill by its flex – and don't let it get wet!
* Read and follow all the safety instructions that come with your drill.

SAFE FiXES
ACCIDENT-AVOIDANCE ACCESSORIES

The first time Kevin visited his local DIY store, the wise old man who works there became alarmed at his evident klutziness. Before he would sell him so much as a light bulb, the old man insisted that Kevin stocked up on safety gear. Here's what he recommended:

IMPACT-RESISTANT CLEAR SAFETY GOGGLES
Essential for any high-speed drilling, cutting or sanding jobs to prevent little specks lodging in your eyes. These are also recommended when you're cutting tiles or using toxic chemicals. Forget them at your peril – eye injuries are one of the most common DIY accidents.

MASKS
To stop you breathing in fine particles or nasty fumes. There are different kinds for different jobs. The dust from some types of man-made board is unpleasant, as are the fumes from most kinds of paint stripper and special adhesives.

PROTECTIVE GLOVES
For use whenever your hands might get damaged. There are different materials to suit different tasks. You may even get a choice of colours!

EAR PROTECTORS
Advisable when you're using power tools for more than a few minutes, such as when sanding a floor. Stripped floorboards look great, but they're not worth going deaf for.

KNEE PROTECTORS
These are worth buying if you're spending a lot of time on your knees, perhaps when laying a new floor. ('Or a new girlfriend,' suggests the Captain.)

PIPE AND CABLE DETECTOR
Don't even think of drilling into walls, floors or ceilings without using one of these first. It will indicate the positions of any gas or water pipes and electric cables lurking behind the plaster. It's also possible to buy triple detectors that can locate concealed nails as well, meaning you wouldn't need the next item on the list...

A STUD FINDER!
Studs are vertical wooden struts found in plasterboard walls. If you're fixing anything remotely heavy to the wall, it's best to fix it into a stud, which is why you need a stud finder. Just hold down the activation switch, slide it over the wall, and a red light will flash when it senses an obstruction behind the plaster (it actually detects the plasterboard nails).

A PORTABLE WORKBENCH
Useful for woodwork, when you need a stable surface to work on. Use clamps to attach wood securely before sawing.

FIRST-AID KIT
Every home should have a basic kit with antiseptic salve, tweezers and plasters.

WHAT TO WEAR
You don't have to buy special overalls – any old clothes will do, so long as they are close-fitting (no flowing Isadora Duncan scarves) and allow you to move easily (forget those skintight jeans). Avoid woolly sweaters when decorating – you wouldn't believe the number of fibres that can stick to a freshly painted wall when you merely brush past it.

Wear sturdy shoes or boots, preferably with reinforced toes, to avoid excruciating pain when hammers are dropped. Note that even professional electricians wear rubber-soled shoes when working on electrical fittings – rubber doesn't conduct electricity so can save you from shocks. Thick rubber soles are also good for working on ladders – and make sure you keep those laces tied.

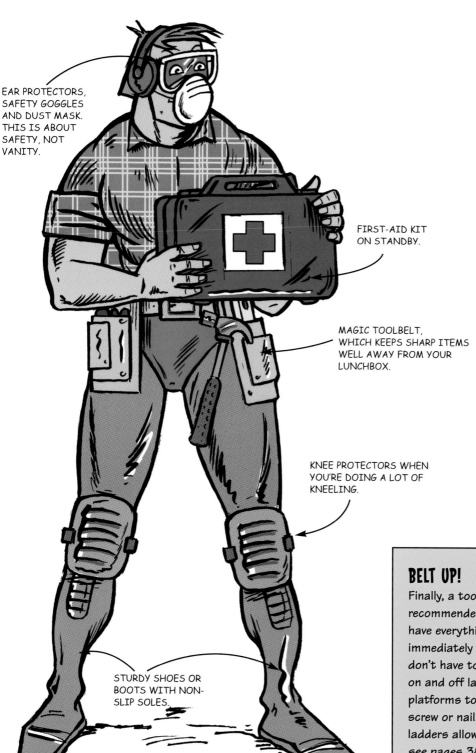

EAR PROTECTORS, SAFETY GOGGLES AND DUST MASK. THIS IS ABOUT SAFETY, NOT VANITY.

FIRST-AID KIT ON STANDBY.

MAGIC TOOLBELT, WHICH KEEPS SHARP ITEMS WELL AWAY FROM YOUR LUNCHBOX.

KNEE PROTECTORS WHEN YOU'RE DOING A LOT OF KNEELING.

STURDY SHOES OR BOOTS WITH NON-SLIP SOLES.

BELT UP!

Finally, a toolbelt is highly recommended, so you have everything you need immediately to hand and don't have to keep hopping on and off ladders and work platforms to locate an extra screw or nail. (No hopping on ladders allowed anyway – see pages 38–9.)

SCREWS, NAILS AND OTHER FIXINGS

There are hundreds of different nails, screws and fixings, with different shapes, lengths, diameters and fixing methods. Here are a few of the most useful types you're likely to come across:

SCREWS

SEE PAGE 26 FOR SCREWING ADVICE!

Screws come with cross-heads (an X shape on top) or slotted heads (a groove on top). Cross-heads are much easier to drive in, especially with an electric screwdriver, so the Captain likes them best.

WOOD SCREWS

The gauge of a screw (from 0 to 20) indicates its diameter, but you can buy screws of the same gauge in a number of different lengths. No. 8 wood screws are the most widely used for general woodworking.

COUNTERSUNK SCREWS

These tighten with the head just below the wood's surface. Get them with slotted or, preferably, cross-shaped heads.

ROUND-HEAD SCREWS

Use these for fixing sheet materials that are too thin to be countersunk.

RAISED-HEAD SCREWS

These are used for decorative fixings, door handle plates and some hinges. They need to be countersunk up to the rim.

CHIPBOARD SCREWS

The threads (twisting ridges) extend right up to the head; for use in chipboard and wood.

COACH SCREWS

Strong fixings; twist them in with a spanner.

WALLPLUGS

These dinky little plastic plugs are needed to hold screws in masonry walls. Match the size of plug to your drill bit and screw. Drill a hole of the correct depth (see page 26) and push the plug into it. When you screw in the screw, the sides of the plug expand outwards and grip the wall firmly.

STRAIGHT PLUGS

These just take the screw thread and have to be cut so they are shorter than the depth of the hole.

MOULDED PLUGS

Have a split at the end, so can take a range of screw lengths.

NAILS

Round-head wire nails are general purpose, but they can split wood if you're not careful.

SEE PAGE 27 FOR SOME HAMMERING ADVICE.

OVAL WIRE NAILS

These will stop your wood splitting if you drive them in with the long-head axis running in the direction of the grain.

LOST-HEAD NAILS

For flooring. The nail head can be driven below the surface with a nail punch.

PANEL PINS

Small heads, easily punched in, for furniture and mouldings. Buy a panel pin punch if the job requires lots of them.

MASONRY NAILS

Good for fixing wood to masonry, but they are permanent (unlike screws, which can be removed).

PLASTERBOARD NAILS

Have a ridged shank for gripping plasterboard.

TACKS

For fixing carpet to wooden floors.

HOLLOW-WALL FIXINGS

These ingenious devices are used for fixing medium loads to plasterboard walls. They are designed so that supports open up on the other side of the board once they are screwed in.

SPRING TOGGLE

A toggle bar folds flat to allow you to insert it, then springs open once inside the wall. It can be used on ceilings, too.

GRAVITY TOGGLE

The toggle drops down when it is inside the wall.

METAL ANCHOR

Metal flaps open out inside the wall. (A plastic anchor is the same, but with plastic flaps.)

KNOCK-DOWN FIXINGS

These are the tricksy bits and pieces you'll find in your flatpack for joining panels and other components together. All of them require that your pieces are lined up exactly.

BLOCK JOINT

For joining boards at right angles. One plastic block is secured to each piece, then the two blocks are screwed together.

CROSS DOWEL

Good for attaching rails or slats to side panels. A metal dowel is inserted through a hole in the side panel, then a screw is slotted into the dowel through a hole in the rail or slat.

ADHESIVES

The only rule is to follow the instructions on the pack. Oh, and make sure your surfaces are clean and dry. And don't glue your fingers together.

PVA (POLYVINYL ACETATE ADHESIVE)

For joining wood and boards.

TWO-PART EPOXY ADHESIVES

The two parts must be mixed together; good for joints that need to be waterproof or very strong.

FLOORING ADHESIVES

Used for sticking floor coverings to floors. They are flexible, so won't crack when you walk on the floor.

COVING AND TILING ADHESIVES

For fixing coving to walls or tiles to floors.

INSTANT-GRAB ADHESIVES

For sticking on wooden skirting boards, or threshold strips in doorways.

SUPERGLUES

Sometimes the only answer for sticking metal, glass, ceramic and plastic. They also stick skin, and a special solvent is needed to remove them.

SOME ADHESIVES GIVE OFF DANGEROUS FUMES, SO KEEP THE AREA WELL VENTILATED AND WEAR A BREATHING MASK IF THE MANUFACTURER RECOMMENDS IT.

A DECORATOR'S TOOLKIT

EXPRESS YOUR CREATIVITY

There are some jobs where you can save money by improvising to make your own tools – and others where cheap is a bad idea. Here's the Captain's rundown on the tools you'll need for stripping, painting, wallpapering and tiling.

STRIPPING (WITH YOUR CLOTHES ON)

STRIPPING KNIFE/SCRAPER

This has a flat, slightly flexible blade (stiffer than a filling knife) that's about 75 mm (3 in) wide. It's essential for stripping old wallpaper and scraping off old paint. Hold the edge flat against the wall so you don't gouge out any plaster.

SHAVEHOOK

A handle with a triangular or pear-shaped blade on the end for scraping paint out of decorative mouldings and other awkward-to-reach places.

HOT-AIR GUN

Like a supercharged hairdryer that softens paint, allowing you to scrape it off. You can attach a nozzle called a spreader to diffuse the heat over a wider area. Don't use it near glass or plastic, though. Not ever. It will crack and melt them.

ORBITAL SCORER

This nifty little tool pierces old washable or painted wallpaper so you can soak and scrape it more efficiently. The alternative is to spend time making little nicks all over the wall with the edge of your scraper, or to hire or buy a steam stripper.

STEAM STRIPPER

If you've got a lot to strip, this will save masses of time. Steam is released through the plate to soften the adhesive holding your paper to the wall. Be sure to read and obey all the safety warnings.

PAINTING (WITHOUT MAKING A MESS)

PAINTBRUSHES

Buy good-quality brushes, as they'll last longer and shed fewer bristles on your paintwork. For smaller areas, 12 mm (½ in), 25 mm (1 in) and 50 mm (2 in) brushes should be all you need. For larger areas, such as walls and ceilings, opt for a 100 mm (4 in) or 150 mm (6 in) brush.

CUTTING-IN BRUSH

Has an angled tip for reaching into difficult crevices and corners. These are invaluable if you're painting window frames or doors with mouldings.

PAINT KETTLE

A small plastic or metal container with a handle. Professional decorators always use these to decant smaller quantities of paint into – much easier to carry around than the whole tin. It also prevents brush-borne dust and debris from contaminating a whole tin of paint. (It's not really a kettle, so don't try to boil water in it.)

PAINTBRUSH CLEANING POTS

Nifty little pots in which you can suspend your brushes in solvent, to clean them without the bristles becoming distorted. Make your own by drilling a hole through the handle of your paintbrush and threading through a thin wire that you can use to suspend it over a jar of solvent (or soapy water – see page 21).

PAINT SHIELD

May be useful for creating neat edges at skirting and coving, or keeping the paint off the glass when you're painting windows. Alternatively, stick masking tape over the edge of the area you want to protect.

GLASS SCRAPER

This gets paint off glass when your paint shield hasn't worked (or if you forgot to use one).

PAINT ROLLERS

Buy a roller handle with several separate sleeves. There are short-pile ones for smooth surfaces, shaggier ones for uneven surfaces, and ones with grooves cut in the surface to produce interesting textures (ooh, luvverly).

ROLLER TRAY

Pour paint into this (but not too much at a time) when using a paint roller. It has a ridged bottom, over which you run the roller back and forwards to get even amounts of paint into the sleeve.

CORNER ROLLER

A dinky one for reaching into corners.

LONG-HANDLED MINI ROLLER

Helps you to paint behind radiators.

ROLLER WITH EXTENSION POLE

For painting ceilings without needing too much of a stretch.

PAINT PADS

These come with disposable pads and their own paint tray. Some people prefer pads to rollers for covering large areas.

WALLPAPERING (DON'T GET STUCK)

PASTING TABLE

An inexpensive, long collapsible table that is just wider than a roll of wallpaper.

PASTE BRUSH

You could use an ordinary 100 mm (4 in) or 150 mm (6 in) paintbrush, but proper paste brushes have more bristles and are softer as well.

PASTE BUCKET

Just tie a piece of string tightly across the top of an ordinary bucket so you can wipe off excess paste from your brush and rest the brush bristles on it between pastings.

PAPERHANGER'S BRUSH

It's definitely worth buying the Real McCoy. This has soft bristles that won't damage the surface of your paper as you smooth it down on to the wall.

PLUMBLINE

A piece of string with a weight on the end will do the trick (*see page 25 for advice on how to use a plumbline*). It's essential when you're wallpapering to get that perfect vertical.

WALLPAPER SCISSORS

Have extra-long blades, making it easier to cut in straight lines. Keep them sharp (*see page 22*) and clean off paste as you go along.

SEAM ROLLER

Use this for getting your seams to lie flat, but not on embossed or fragile types of wallpaper, as it could flatten or tear them.

TILING (WITHOUT BREAKING A NAIL)

TILE SCORER

To make thin tiles easier to cut or snap, run a scorer along your marked cutting line.

HEAVY-DUTY TILE CUTTER

A combined jig and cutter for shaping thicker wall and floor tiles.

TILE SAW

A saw for cutting curves in tiles that have to fit around pipework or other rounded obstructions.

NIPPERS

Nibble away little pieces of tile with these. They're often used with mosaic tiles.

THE RIGHT STUFF

ELECTRIC TILE CUTTER
if you're doing a lot of tiling, you'll be grateful for one of these. Oh, yes!

TILE FILE
Removes rough edges from cut tiles.

PROFILE GAUGE
An optional extra for helping to cut your tiles to the exact shape for fitting around obstructions. A cardboard template is almost as good (but much fiddlier).

NOTCHED SPREADER
There are different kinds for wall and floor tiles, but both have notches designed to spread your adhesive to the correct thickness.

GROUT SPREADER
As the name suggests, these are for spreading grout. Once again, there are different kinds for wall tiles and floor tiles.

GROUT SHAPER
A little plastic tool with interchangeable heads for smoothing your grout joints into neat shapes. You could use a flat wooden lollipop stick instead.

CLEANING YOUR DECORATING TOOLS

WATER-BASED PAINTS
Brushes, pads and rollers can be cleaned in a solution of normal household detergent. Wipe off excess paint on to a piece of newspaper, then swish your tools around in the soapy water. If any paint has dried in the bristles, remove it with an old nailbrush. Rinse the brushes in clean water. Professional decorators then stand their brushes for 20 minutes in a container of warm water with a scoosh of hair conditioner to stop the bristles becoming brittle. However, don't leave the brushes standing on their bristles, which could distort them. Suspend them from a wire across the rim of the container, or buy a special paint cleaning pot (*see page 19*). Afterwards, hang brushes up to dry. When storing them, wrap an elastic band around the bristles to keep them in shape.

SOLVENT-BASED PAINTS
These need to be removed with white spirit or proprietary brush cleaner. Wipe off the excess paint, then swish tools around in a container of solvent, or leave them suspended for a while. Keep repeating the process in clean solvent until the brush is clean, then rinse it in warm soapy water and condition, as for water-based paints. It can take a long time to clean a roller sleeve of emulsion paint, especially a solvent-based one. The Captain's advice is to keep one sleeve for white paint only, and just throw the others away after use.

WALLPAPER PASTE
Wash brushes, rollers and any tools that have come into contact with wallpaper paste in warm soapy water.

GROUT
Wipe excess grout off straight away with a damp sponge. It's a cement-based product, so if it dries on tools or tiles, you'll have to chip it off later. It can leave a white smeary film on the surface of tiles, but this will wipe off relatively easily with a dry cloth.

LOOKING AFTER YOUR TOOLS
AND KEEPING THEM TIDY

EVEN IF YOU'RE NOT THE SHARPEST KNIFE IN THE DRAWER, YOU CAN STILL HAVE THE BEST-HONED CHISEL IN YOUR TOOLBOX.

Not only will tools last much longer if you clean, care for and store them properly – they could also be dangerous to use if you don't.

CUTTING TOOLS

Blunt cutting tools can slip and cause accidents. Keep them sharp and throw away disposable blades as soon as they stop cutting smoothly. Store sharp tools with care – don't throw them willy-nilly into a toolbox, where they'll cut your hand next time you dip in. Fit blade guards to saws, knives and chisels whenever they're not in use.

Have saws professionally sharpened from time to time. Hang them from dowelling pegs on a wall, with protective covers across their teeth, to stop the blades from warping.

Chisels and planes can be sharpened on an oilstone block lubricated with a little oil. Use a gadget called a honing guide to hold the blade in place and rub it to and fro on the oilstone until a burr is raised, then turn the blade over and repeat. Make a rack for storing chisels so that they can hang with the blades pointing downwards. Planes should be stored on their sides and never placed face-down – take them apart and clean the blades before long-term storage.

Worn flathead screwdriver tips can also benefit from being rubbed on an oilstone, then having their ends squared with a metal file.

To clean a metal file, rub it with a wire brush, then coat the teeth with chalk to prevent it clogging up so quickly next time.

It is possible to sharpen drill bits, but it's best to have it done professionally – or just buy replacements. Remove the blade from power jigsaws after use.

> **CAPTAIN'S TIP**
> Tools with wooden handles should be protected from damp and also from drying out. Too much damp will cause the wood to swell and crack, while too much dryness can cause it to shrink.

CLEANING UP

It may be as boring as your mother telling you to tidy your bedroom, but the truth is that if you clean your tools as you go along, it will be much, much easier. Dried-on plaster, adhesive, grout, wallpaper paste and paint will make tools less accurate and more accident-prone. Once plaster or grout has dried, it can only be chipped or sanded off tools. If you catch them before they dry, they can be rinsed off under running water.

To remove adhesives, check the solvent that is recommended on the packaging. It might simply be water or methylated spirit, or you may have to buy a proprietary solvent.

There was advice about cleaning off paint and wallpaper paste from brushes and rollers earlier on (*see page 21*). Use the same methods for cleaning them from tools – but if they've dried, you're going to need serious elbow grease or the right solvent! Either that or it's time to buy some new tools.

Follow the manufacturer's instructions when disposing of caustic chemicals, like paint strippers. It is against the law to flush some types of chemical into water courses, because they can cause ecological damage. Check with your local authority how they would like you to dispose of oil paint, aerosols, white spirit, varnish and wood stains.

Place broken glass into strong cardboard boxes, tape them up and mark 'Broken glass' on the outside. Don't risk injuring your poor old refuse disposal team when they come to collect them.

Store all toxic substances out of the reach of children and animals, and never decant them into unlabelled bottles. Someone somewhere might mistake them for a new kind of lemonade.

BEING TIDY

Put away each tool as soon as you've finished with it, even in the middle of a job. If nothing else, it'll be one less item that you can trip over. Toolboxes are handy for keeping everything together. Choose ones with lots of individual storage drawers in which you can keep different sizes of screws, nails and fixings, so that you're not caught, mid-project, rummaging around for half an hour trying to find a No. 8 countersunk wood screw. Transfer the items you will need for each part of a task into your toolbelt and you'll be well on the way to becoming a Captain Competent yourself!

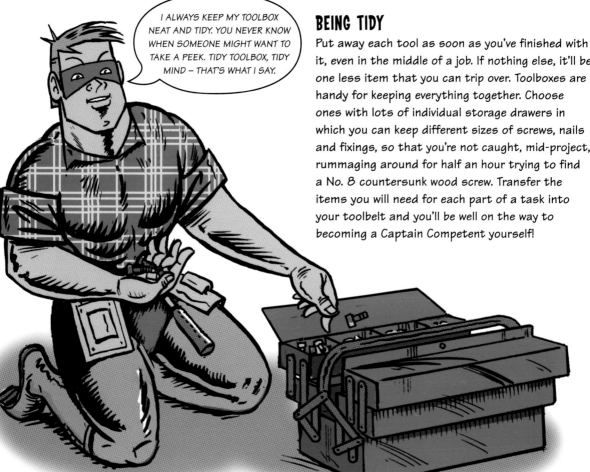

I ALWAYS KEEP MY TOOLBOX NEAT AND TIDY. YOU NEVER KNOW WHEN SOMEONE MIGHT WANT TO TAKE A PEEK. TIDY TOOLBOX, TIDY MIND – THAT'S WHAT I SAY.

10 BASIC TECHNIQUES
THE ABC OF DIY

1. MASTERFUL MEASURING

Never assume that corners are right angles; never believe that verticals are true; never trust that horizontal surfaces are flat. Look at the room you're in right now – I bet you anything that the distance between the ceiling and floor will be slightly different at different points. Buildings settle over the years, and some subside. Building materials expand and contract in heat and cold, or at different levels of humidity. All these things are sent to try conscientious DIYers – but fortunately there are ways to check and correct most anomalies.

SO TRUE

Don't forget the old-timers' measuring mantra: 'Measure twice, cut once.'

STEEL RULE

Use a retractable steel rule to measure longer distances, like the length and width of a room. Take your measurements at several points, and make a scale plan if they are substantially different. Don't forget to allow for the length of the tape measure body if you're taking interior measurements – it will be marked on the casing. For shorter lengths, a 610 mm (2 ft) steel rule is useful, and will also double as a straightedge.

TRY SQUARE

A try square with a fixed blade measures and marks right angles; combination squares can be used to mark 45° angles as well, and some incorporate a basic spirit level.

To measure irregular angles inside alcoves, you can use a nifty tool called a sliding bevel – you just rest the bevel on one wall, then open out the blade to lie along the adjacent one, and there's your angle in black and white (or black on silver).

SPIRIT LEVEL

Spirit levels come in a variety of lengths and should have bubbles set in at least two vials to show horizontals and verticals. When the bubble is centred in relation to the markings on the horizontal vial, the surface is level. Ditto verticals. Some even have a third bubble for measuring 45° angles. Whatever will they think of next? Always recheck your horizontals and verticals after hammering or drilling, in case you've knocked anything out of alignment.

PLUMBLINE

When you need to mark a straight vertical down a long distance, like a wall, a plumbline should be your chosen tool. Buy one or make your own by attaching a weight to a piece of string. There are no magic tricks – they work by gravity – but check that the string is hanging freely because if it touches a bump in the wall, it could hang off line.

SCALE PLANS

Write your measurements clearly on a piece of paper and remember to take it to the DIY store with you. If they are more complicated than simple height, width and depth, you would be well advised to make a drawing of the area you are working on –

preferably to scale on squared graph paper – and take that along too. For example, if you're planning a new fitted kitchen, you need a scale plan to check those important little details like whether you've left enough room for cupboard doors to swing open, or if the washing machine will fit.

The measurements in this book are given in metric, with imperial equivalents in brackets afterwards. Whatever you do, don't confuse the two or you could find that you've only bought enough carpet to make a doormat, yet enough tiles to retile the floors of the town hall.

To mark fixing positions on walls, wood, cupboards or tiles, there are different ideal methods. Where it won't show, or can be rubbed off afterwards, use a hard pencil (soft ones give fatter lines, which are less accurate). On wood, use a sharp craft knife.

To mark wall tiles for cutting, use a water-soluble felt pen, but on more porous tiling, a chinagraph pen is the implement of choice for making your mark.

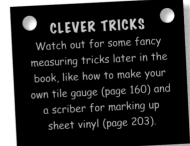

CLEVER TRICKS
Watch out for some fancy measuring tricks later in the book, like how to make your own tile gauge (page 160) and a scriber for marking up sheet vinyl (page 203).

DO YOU LIKE MY BIG TOWER? LET ME EXPLAIN HOW TO SCREW – WITHOUT SCREWING UP.

2. SUCCESSFUL SCREWING

Screws fix wood together more firmly than nails, and the great advantage is that they can be unscrewed again if need be.

First of all, use a screwdriver that fits the size of the screw head – too wide a blade will slip out, and too narrow a blade could mangle up the slot. Place the blade square in the slot and turn clockwise to screw, anticlockwise to unscrew. Simple as that? Well, no, not always...

You may need to drill a pilot hole before inserting your screw to help it go in more easily. If you're joining one piece of wood to another, you'll need to drill a <u>clearance hole</u> through the first material and a <u>pilot hole</u> in the second. Remember those terms – they'll crop up time and again. There's a simple rule of thumb for judging the diameter of hole needed (and thus the size of drill bit required): clearance holes should be the diameter of the screw shank and pilot holes are half its diameter. You can use a bradawl to make holes for screws that are smaller than gauge 6.

The length of screws needed for each job will depend on the materials being joined. If you're joining two pieces of wood, the screws will need to be long enough to go right through the first piece and halfway through the second. To insert screws into masonry walls, use long screws and plugs for good penetration – at least 38 mm (1½ in) or even 50 mm (2 in) plus the thickness of the wood you are fixing. With shelving and picture hanging, the heavier the weight that the screws need to support, the longer they should be.

Remember that you'll need a countersink drill bit to make holes for countersunk screws. They create a shallow crater that the screw head can sit in. After inserting the screw, fill the crater with wood filler and sand it down when dry for an ultra-professional superhero finish.

THERE'S THRILLING DRILLING ADVICE ON PAGES 28–9.

3. HAPPY HAMMERING

To drive in a nail, hold it perpendicular to the surface, tap it gently with a hammer until it has engaged, then take your hand away. Hold the hammer near the end of the handle and swing your forearm from the elbow, letting the weight of the head drop the hammer, and keep tapping until your nail is sufficiently sunk in. Piece of cake, eh? So why have most veteran DIYers suffered a blackened thumb nail at some stage in their careers? Here are a few tips so you can avoid their fate:

* Don't use a hammer that's too heavy for the job in hand.
* Keep your hammer head clean and free of grease. Rub it on a piece of fine abrasive paper from time to time.
* Start small nails using the cross-peen end (the smaller end) of a cross-peen hammer and, if you can't hold them straight with your fingers, try using a pair of pincers.
* Alternatively, push tiny panel pins through a stiff piece of paper, hold them by the paper, drive them in then, when the pin is almost home, tear the paper away.
* Note that nails don't work well in chipboard – use chipboard screws instead.

* If you want to drive your nails below the surface, finish off the job with a nail punch.
* Keep your eyes on the job at all times. Many injuries result from distractions just at the crucial part of a hammer swing.

HOW TO REMOVE NAILS

Hook the nail head with the claw end of a claw hammer and pull. To avoid damaging the surface of the wood, place a thin piece of card or wood under the hammer and pull it straight out from the surface. For a long nail, replace the card with blocks of wood of ever-increasing depth as the nail begins to come out.

If the nail has lost its head, grip it with a pair of pliers. Once again, place a piece of card between the pliers and the wood surface to avoid damaging it. To remove tacks from an old carpet, it helps to use a special tool called a tack lifter.

NAILING SECRETS

There are some sophisticated nailing techniques described later. See page 125 for tips on secret nailing, and page 188 for a method called 'skewing'!

4. DISASTER-FREE DRILLING

If you're new to electric drills, practise your techniques on some offcuts of wood before you go near anything of value – like your walls; or a brand-new flatpack; or your spanking state-of-the-art kitchen units.

First of all, read the manufacturer's instructions to see how a drill bit is fitted in the chuck. Most drills now have automatic chuck locking, but if yours doesn't, turn the key in one of the three holes so that the jaws make firm contact with the bit.

Always drill perpendicular to the surface – horizontally into a wall, or vertically into a piece of wood clamped on a work bench. You can buy drill guides to keep the drill straight, but this is only worthwhile if you're doing a lot of drilling. Otherwise, if you're drilling into a horizontal

surface, you could position a try square next to the drill and keep them parallel.

It's a good idea to make a starter hole with a bradawl, so the drill doesn't slide off to the side. Place the drill bit in the starter hole, make sure you have everything lined up, then start drilling at a slow speed. Once you can feel that the bit has penetrated the surface, you can increase the speed – but don't force it to go too fast. Let the drill do the work.

Hold the drill firmly with both hands. If you hit a knot in the wood, there can sometimes be kick-back and you don't want to risk dropping it. When you switch the drill off, wait until it has fully stopped before laying it down – or you could find it propelling itself mysteriously across the floor.

JOINING WOOD

Let's say you're joining two pieces of softwood with a No. 8 wood screw. Decide what length of screw you will need by measuring the depth of the top piece and half the depth of the second, then add them together. For the clearance hole, choose a drill bit that's the same diameter as the shank of the screw. For the pilot hole, choose one half that diameter. If you want the screw to be countersunk, choose a countersink bit and screw.

You have to drill the clearance hole all the way through the top piece of wood. Position it with the side that will be on show facing upwards and clamp an offcut of wood underneath, then drill until you can feel that you have broken through the top piece. Remove the clamp.

Now you have to drill a pilot hole in the second piece of wood. Change your drill bit for one half the diameter and fit a depth stop on the bit that is half the depth of the second bit of wood. You can buy plastic guides, but the easiest kind of depth stop is a piece of masking tape stuck at the correct height around the bit. Simply drill until your tape meets the surface of the wood.

Finally, put the first piece on top of the second, line up the holes and screw in your screw. Tarrah! The wood is joined.

DRILLING INTO MASONRY WALLS

Check the walls with a pipe and cable detector to make sure there are no buried pipes or cables and mark your fixing position. It can help if you make a small starter hole with a bradawl. Choose your screws and plugs and mark a depth stop on the drill bit that is slightly deeper than the length of the plug.

It's easiest to drill into masonry with your drill set to hammer action (which is up to three times faster than standard action), but if you are not experienced with drills, start at a slow speed without hammer action turned on. Hold the drill perpendicular to the wall and keep it steady – or your hole will have tapered edges! Pull the bit out of the hole every 30 seconds or so to clear away any dust and debris, then continue.

Stop drilling when you reach the depth stop. Your wallplug should tap in easily. Use a hammer to sink it to the level of the wall if finger pressure alone doesn't work.

MAKING BIG HOLES IN WOOD

To make holes with a diameter of 12 to 38 mm (½ in to 1½ in), you should use an appropriate flat drill bit. Start on one side of the wood and drill through until the tip of the bit has just penetrated. Then work from the other side to finish off the hole neatly, with no splintering around the edges.

There are more drilling tips throughout the book (*see page 70 for advice on drilling into tiles*). And don't forget that safety advice on page 13!

DOWN, BOY! DON'T USE FAST SPEEDS OR HAMMER ACTION UNTIL YOU'RE CONFIDENT YOU CAN CONTROL YOUR DRILL.

5. CAREFUL CUTTING

Captain's tip number one: whenever possible get your local DIY store or timber yard to cut wood to the correct length for you. This saves hassle, and their sophisticated power saws will probably give cleaner edges than you would manage yourself. If you have to cut wood to length at home, do it slowly and carefully, following all the handy sawing tips given here.

SAWING IN STRAIGHT LINES

First of all, make sure you're sober. Don't try sawing when you've been partaking of the old super-refreshments. That would be silly and, of course, the Captain would never consider it. Clamp the wood you are cutting to a workbench, and measure and mark your cutting line. Hold the saw with your index finger extending down the handle to steady it. Place the cutting edge of the saw just to the waste side of your cutting line – if you cut along the line, your wood will be slightly too short. Rest the thumb of your free hand against the side of the blade, to support it, and begin the cut by pulling the saw backwards. Use the full length of the blade and exert light pressure on the forwards stroke, then slide it back again. Keep an eye on both sides to make sure you're not wandering off at a tangent. If your saw is sharp enough, it should glide through wood fairly easily.

Whenever you're drilling or cutting wood, work down from the side that will be on display – unless you're using a power saw. Power saw teeth cut upwards, so you should work with the underside of the wood or board (the bit that won't be on show) facing down so that the cleanest, smartest surface will be on the top.

If you are cutting through a large board rather than a single plank, support it between two sawhorses, or steady surfaces of the same height, and clamp it in place. If you have trouble following a long cutting line, try clamping a wooden batten along the line and using it as your guide.

Man-made boards with melamine coating or wood veneer are extremely prone to chipping. For best results, score along the cutting line with a craft knife, using a straightedge to keep you straight. Then use a fine-toothed saw, such as a tenon saw, and work so that the side that will show is facing upwards.

As you get towards the end of your cut, hold on to the waste piece with one hand or the wood could splinter as its weight pulls it downwards. If this is hard to do, you could walk around and finish the cut from the other side of your wood.

DON'T LET YOUR PADSAW SLIP OR IT MIGHT MAKE YOUR CIRCLE VICIOUS.

CHISELS ARE DANGEROUS AND SHOULD BE TREATED WITH RESPECT. ISN'T THAT RIGHT, SIR?

USING A PADSAW

There will be times when you need to cut shapes from a wooden panel – for example, if you're making keyholes in a door. That's when your trusty padsaw comes into the limelight. Start by drilling a hole or holes in the waste part of the wood until there is enough room to insert the tip of your padsaw. Follow the cutting line, then file the edges smooth afterwards. To cut out a keyhole, drill a large hole above, a small one below, then join them with a couple of strokes of the padsaw.

USING A CHISEL

Chisels have many uses, but one of their invaluable tricks is cutting shallow recesses in doors to take hinges, locks and latches. Don't use the chisel to gouge out chunks of wood – it should merely shave off slivers.

Make sure the wood is secured so it can't move and mark out the area you want to remove. Cut around the edges of the area by holding the chisel with its bevelled cutting edge facing into the area you're cutting out and pushing it firmly into the wood.

Now hold the chisel horizontally, with the bevel facing up, and move it around each side, working towards the centre of the area. If hand pressure

alone isn't working, tap the end of the chisel gently with a hammer or mallet. Whatever you do, don't rest the other hand in front of the chisel blade, because if it slips, you'll get a nasty cut.

When you reach the bottom of the area, shave it with the chisel until it is smooth.

CAPTAIN'S TIP

You can also trim wood with a plane. See over the page if you fancy a bit of planing... And for advice on buying wood, see pages 126-7.

SAFETY WITH JIGSAWS

Before you switch on a jigsaw, check that the blade is securely fitted in place, and keep checking that it hasn't worked loose as you do your cutting. Always remove the blade to store the jigsaw when you've finished. Wear goggles to avoid getting sawdust in your eyes, and gloves to protect your hands from the blade, which can get hot while you work. Adjust the soleplate to sit on the surface of the wood; note that some will allow you to cut at an angle. Fit an RCD to the power socket (see page 28) just in case you accidentally cut through the jigsaw cable. No, of course you wouldn't!

It's easy to get carried away. The shavings look so-o-o cute 'n' curly.

6. SOPHISTICATED SMOOTHING

There are some things in life you just want to be smooth – hollandaise sauce, bed sheets and skin spring to mind. Oh, and any wooden surfaces that you have to touch, sit on or walk on. Here are a few tips on getting your wood beautifully smooth. For advice on your hollandaise, buy a cookery book.

USING A PLANE

Planes are great for trimming and smoothing wood, and for straightening irregular edges if your cutting has gone a bit wonky, but they are difficult for beginners to use, so practise on some offcuts of wood first.

Insert a sharp blade in the base of your plane by lifting the lever to release the wedge iron and cap iron. Screw the blade and cap iron together so that the cap iron is roughly 2 mm (1/16 in) in from the cutting edge, and the cap is on the non-bevelled side of the blade. Place them bevel-side down in your plane, engage the adjusting lever, then put the lever cap over the central screw and bring the wedge lever down.

Turn the depth adjustment knob so that the blade is just protruding. Make sure the edge of the blade is parallel to the surface of the plane, then try it out. If the cut is too deep or too shallow,

adjust until you've got it right. Clamp the wood that is being planed securely in place, then press down on the front of the plane as you move it along the wood in the direction of the grain. At the end of each stroke, release the pressure on the front to move it back to the starting position.

Never plane against or across the grain or you'll make a right old pig's breakfast of your wood. You should be producing even ribbons of wood shavings. Use a spirit level to make sure you are planing the edge level and keep checking the depth so you don't trim off too much.

SANDING WITH ABRASIVE PAPERS

Abrasive papers finish the surface of the wood while only reducing it in size very slightly, much less than planes do. Wrap your paper around a cork sanding block and rub it along the grain of the wood. Start with a coarse grade and move on to medium, then fine. It can be a good idea to raise the grain of the wood before the final sanding by dampening it, then letting it dry.

You can buy or hire power sanders if there's a lot of sanding to do, and some electric drills can take sanding attachments (*see pages 106–9 for advice on sanding floorboards and pages 210–11 for information on Caroline's chest. Hey, hey!*).

7. TRIMMING TILES

No matter how carefully you plan the layout of your tiles, you will inevitably have to cut some to fit edges and corners, and perhaps to curve around intransigent obstacles like windows, basins and WCs. Wear safety goggles to prevent any tile shards getting into your eyes.

SCORING AND SNAPPING

The most straightforward way to cut straight lines in tiles is with a tile scorer. Mark your cutting line on the face of the tile, place a steel rule alongside it, then run the hardened tip of the scorer firmly along the cutting line. Place a pencil underneath the cutting line, press down on the tile on each side and it should snap cleanly in two. If it doesn't, you may need to run the scorer down the cutting line again, but this is not ideal. Try to score and snap in single decisive movements to get the cleanest cuts.

If you've got loads of tiles to cut, then it's worth investing in a tile cutting machine. It uses the same principle of scoring and snapping, but the tile is inserted into a jig and lined up with the tool's guide before you push a handle to score the tile. The handle is then pulled down firmly over the tile to snap it.

Hard floor tiles are thicker than ceramic wall tiles, so you may need to buy or hire a heavy-duty tile cutter. The operating method is much the same, but you might decide to ask your personal superhero for a bit of help.

CUTTING CURVES

It's very inconvenient that bathroom fittings aren't square or rectangular, but it can't be helped. Make a cardboard template of the curves, then use it to mark your cutting line on the tiles. Use a clamp to hold the tile firmly in position before you cut around the curve with a tile saw. Work slowly to avoid chipping the glaze. If any tiny adjustments need to be made, such as cutting off a corner or removing a sliver from an edge, you can do this with tile nibblers. Score with a tile scorer first, then nibble away the excess little pieces.

FILING

Finish off cut edges with a tile file. Hold it square to the edge of the tile and move from the glazed direction downwards. Not back and forwards or side to side – just down.

GETTING LAID
Find everything else you'll need to know about tiling on pages 160-9.

I USE FAST-SETTING FILLER WHEN I'M RUNNING LATE FOR A HOT DATE.

8. PERFECT PLASTERING

The truth is that plastering is an art that can take a lifetime to master. If you have a large area to be plastered, it's well worth hiring a professional (*see page 216*). Unless you're happy to live with bumps and curves and crumbly flaky bits that will compromise every finish you try to lay on top. Oh, and you'll have a field day trying to fix shelves and cupboards to uneven walls.

Having said all that, it's useful to know the basics of plastering so you can fill in little cracks and holes yourself — and if you're just beginning your DIY career, you're bound to create a few of these along the way...

TYPES OF FILLER

Professionals use a base coat, then a finishing coat on top. Made of gypsum, their plaster is quick-drying and very tricky to use. Even Captain Competent has trouble with this. If you have a large hole or a deep crack to fill, try one-coat plasters instead — they're more expensive, but slower to dry, giving you more time to get them smooth and even.

For small repairs, you just need the correct kind of filler. Buy a tub of general-purpose cellulose filler, which will either be ready-mixed or a powder to which you have to add water. This will do for most cracks and holes up to 13 mm (½ in) deep. For holes that are up to 25 mm (1 in) deep, you can apply a couple of coats of deep-repair plaster, or you could try using self-adhesive mesh repair tape and a skim coat of filler.

There are a few specialist fillers you might consider as well:
* flexible filler, also known as mastic or caulk, for gaps where wood meets plaster, i.e. around doors, windows, skirting or coving;
* fine-surface filler for a perfect finish on tiny dents or imperfections;
* expanding foam filler for filling gaping holes;
* fast-setting filler, which dries in 10 to 20 minutes, for when you want to press on with your decorating.

CAPTAIN'S TIP
Don't mix more plaster or filler than you can use in about 20 minutes. If it starts to set, you'll have to discard it and mix a new batch.

PLASTERING TOOLS

If you have a lot of plastering to do, it's worth buying or borrowing some proper plastering tools – a trowel, hawk and decorator's float. The correct technique is to pick up some plaster on the hawk, then use the trowel to cut away about half of it. Hold the trowel at an angle to the wall and apply the plaster with upwards vertical strokes, pressing it firmly into the surface. Smooth it down with a decorator's float, then use the edge of your trowel to score a diamond pattern in the surface to provide a good key for the next plaster coat. Let it dry for the requisite time (read the packet, silly!), then apply the finishing coat and smooth it down.

See pages 56–7, where the Captain explains how to fill a small crack in plaster, and then a larger hole in a lath-and-plaster wall. If your hole or crack is more than 25 mm (1 in) deep, get help quick! Your house could be falling down!

FIXING HOLES IN PLASTERBOARD WALLS

To fix a hole in a plasterboard wall, you'll need to insert a replacement patch of plasterboard. Cut a patch that's slightly bigger than your hole (but not so big that it won't fit sideways through the hole) and drill through the centre so you can insert a piece of string through it. Tie a nail to the string at the back (the grey side) of the plasterboard patch, to anchor it in position.

Apply a layer of filler to the front (the white side) of your patch, then manoeuvre it carefully through the hole in the wall and pull on the string to get it into the right position. Keep holding the string taut as you apply more filler over the hole, smoothing it nice and flat.

When the filler has set, you can cut the string flush with the wall and smooth it down with abrasive paper. Paint over the patch to finish off your repair – it'll be good as new (well, almost).

BUMPS-A-DAISY

Shine a light obliquely across the wall to check for any bumps and smooth them before the top coat sets – don't try to sand down plaster or you'll just make a mess.

9. PAINLESS PAINTING

Drips, streaks, blisters, cracks, bristles and wrinkles – these aren't what we want on our paintwork. For a perfect, blemish-free finish, there are no shortcuts – just a few golden rules that have to be followed to the letter. You'll find loads more advice on buying paints and brushes on pages 136–7, and you can see how Kevin gets on with painting his sitting room.

* Choose the right kind of paint for your surface (*see page 136*). Stir it well before use and keep it clean while you work by using a paint kettle.

* Prepare the surface thoroughly (*see pages 138–41*), making sure you apply a good-quality primer that's compatible with your paint; read the manufacturer's instructions, or ask someone helpful in your DIY store.

* Use clean brushes and tools, and don't overload them with paint.

* Don't let humans or animals brush against paint while it's drying. That means you, Kevin! Remove flies, bristles and cat hairs while the paint is still wet, then brush over the area.

BASIC BRUSHWORK

Hold the paintbrush with your thumb on one side and fingers on the other. Dip the brush into the paint to cover about one-third of the bristle depth, then press it against the rim to get rid of any excess. Work on an area of not more than a sq metre (sq yard), moving the brush horizontally and vertically to cover it, then levelling with a basic back and forwards motion. Load the brush again then start another area about a metre (yard) below and work back to the wet edge of the first patch, allowing the paint to merge. Keep working on adjoining areas in the same way, but merging wet edges before they have time to dry. Finish a whole wall before taking a break, or you could find a visible seam where you stopped for that cuppa.

OIL PAINT TECHNIQUES

Oil paints are usually used on woodwork rather than walls or ceilings. Start by making three parallel vertical stripes about 600 mm (2 ft) long that are not quite the width of the brush. Then paint horizontally across the stripes, smoothing them out. Don't reload the brush (it should be almost dry by now) and brush lightly over the section with vertical strokes again. Begin the next section and blend in so that the edges don't show.

BASIC ROLLER AND PAD-WORK

Move the roller up and down its ridged paint tray to get even coverage of paint. Work in a similar way to the brushwork techniques described opposite, but paint large 'W's or 'M's with the roller, without lifting it off the wall, then fill in each section by working it back and forwards. Don't try to push your roller up to edges – there are some special techniques for this...

If you prefer to use paint pads, take care that you load them evenly, and move them up and down in areas about four times the width of the pad. Your movements should be almost like scrubbing – but gentler.

FEELING EDGY

Paint the edges of walls either before or after you've done the main central area. Paint several horizontal strokes from the corner to the edge of the painted area, then make a long vertical brush stroke over the top. This nifty little technique is known as 'cutting in'.

If you reach an edge where the colour changes on an adjoining wall or at the ceiling, you'll have to master another trick, known as 'beading'. Load your brush and press it to the wall, just slightly away from the edge, letting the bristles splay out.

Pull the brush along in a continuous line, working up closer to the edge. If you're careful, you'll get a neat, clear line. If you don't feel confident enough to try this, though, you might want to use an implement known as a paint shield (see page 143) or masking tape.

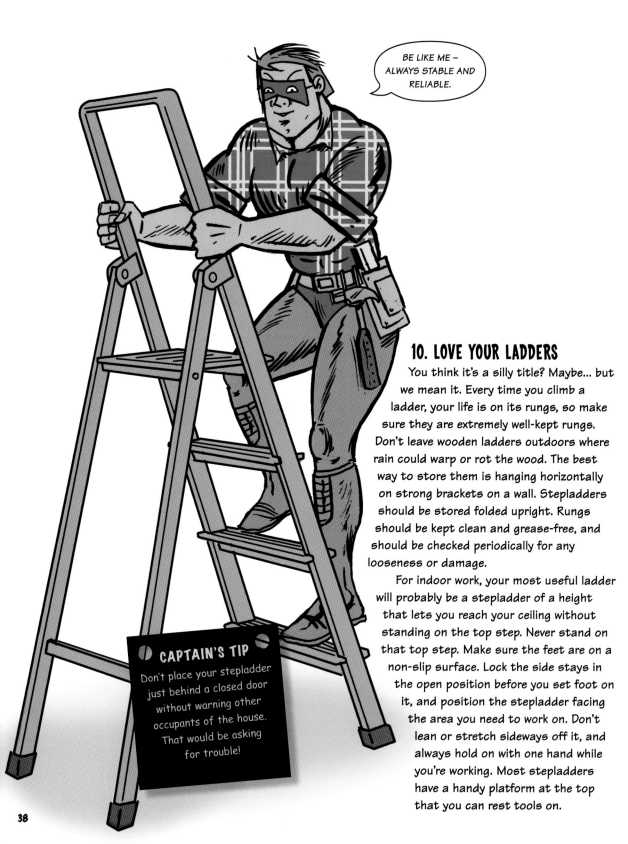

BE LIKE ME – ALWAYS STABLE AND RELIABLE.

10. LOVE YOUR LADDERS

You think it's a silly title? Maybe... but we mean it. Every time you climb a ladder, your life is on its rungs, so make sure they are extremely well-kept rungs. Don't leave wooden ladders outdoors where rain could warp or rot the wood. The best way to store them is hanging horizontally on strong brackets on a wall. Stepladders should be stored folded upright. Rungs should be kept clean and grease-free, and should be checked periodically for any looseness or damage.

For indoor work, your most useful ladder will probably be a stepladder of a height that lets you reach your ceiling without standing on the top step. Never stand on that top step. Make sure the feet are on a non-slip surface. Lock the side stays in the open position before you set foot on it, and position the stepladder facing the area you need to work on. Don't lean or stretch sideways off it, and always hold on with one hand while you're working. Most stepladders have a handy platform at the top that you can rest tools on.

CAPTAIN'S TIP

Don't place your stepladder just behind a closed door without warning other occupants of the house. That would be asking for trouble!

WORK PLATFORMS

If you've got a large area of ceiling to paint and don't want to be jumping up and down repositioning your stepladder all day, you could consider hiring a work platform from your local DIY store. Some combination ladders convert into low-level work platforms with a board stretched between two sections of ladder. You can also hire towers made of light aluminium that frame a work platform with a guard rail around it. These have lockable wheels and stabilizers (for outdoor work) that must be used before you climb it, and are by far the safest option.

Alternatively, for work on high ceilings and areas like stairwells, you can position scaffold boards between two stepladders, or a stepladder and a ladder, in combinations that give you a level surface to stand on. If the distance between your two supports is more than 1.5 m (5 ft), add an extra board on top, to stop them sagging in the middle, and clamp them securely together. If the span is more than 3 m (10 ft), you'll definitely need to add that extra support in the middle. (*See how the Captain designs a stairwell work platform on page 158.*) Always test your work platform verr-r-y carefully before leaping up with paintpot in hand.

If one of your scaffold boards is resting on a ladder, make sure you observe the one-in-four rule. Never heard of it? It's a simple formula for getting the correct angle of lean. If your ladder is 3.6m (12 ft) long, the feet should be positioned a quarter of that distance out from the wall – in other words, 0.9 m (3 ft). One in four. Get it?

SOME FINAL LADDER TIPS

* Don't lean sideways or backwards from the ladder. Keep your centre of gravity inside the stiles (the bits up the sides) at all times.
* Don't climb a ladder with your hands full of tools. What do you think tool-belts are for?
* Wear sensible shoes with thick gripping soles. Stilettos would be plain silly.
* Cordless power tools are safer for working on ladders. Remember that aluminium ladders could conduct electricity!
* If possible, hold on with one hand while you work.
* Oh, yes – and take care!

CAPTAIN COMPETENT'S
EASY FIXES

When we talk about 'Easy Fixes', we mean the kind of home repair that any semi-competent adult should be able to manage by themselves without recourse to the professionals. These are simple remedies for common problems, using basic tools that most people would have to hand. However, Kevin realizes he had better put on the magic toolbelt before attempting to go anywhere near that broken window...

KAPOW

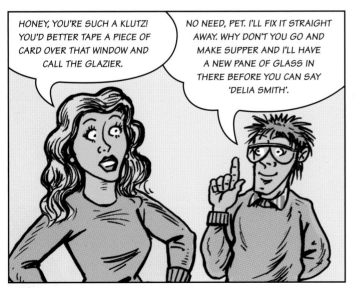

HONEY, YOU'RE SUCH A KLUTZ! YOU'D BETTER TAPE A PIECE OF CARD OVER THAT WINDOW AND CALL THE GLAZIER.

NO NEED, PET. I'LL FIX IT STRAIGHT AWAY. WHY DON'T YOU GO AND MAKE SUPPER AND I'LL HAVE A NEW PANE OF GLASS IN THERE BEFORE YOU CAN SAY 'DELIA SMITH'.

HAVING A SMASHING TIME

HOW TO FIX A BROKEN WINDOW

1 The Captain removes the broken glass from the frame. He hammers gently to loosen each piece, then wiggles it out and lifts it carefully into a cardboard box.

2 Use a hammer and chisel to cut out the old putty from inside the rebate before taking your measurements. Work gently or you could splinter the wood. When you come across little glazing nails (also known as sprigs), remove them with a pair of pliers.

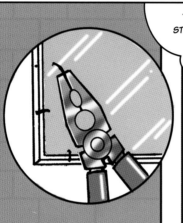

> THERE ARE STILL LITTLE SPLINTERS OF GLASS STUCK IN THE PUTTY. I'M WEARING THESE STYLISH PROTECTIVE GLOVES SO I DON'T CUT MYSELF WHILE I'M CHIPPING THEM OUT.

3 When measuring the size of the pane, allow enough to fit into the rebates. Measure each diagonal to make sure the shape is regular. For a slightly-out-of-square frame, measure all four sides of the rebate. On out-of-square rebates, subtract 3 mm (⅛ in) from the smaller measurement of height and width.

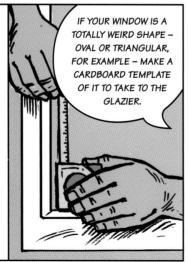

> IF YOUR WINDOW IS A TOTALLY WEIRD SHAPE – OVAL OR TRIANGULAR, FOR EXAMPLE – MAKE A CARDBOARD TEMPLATE OF IT TO TAKE TO THE GLAZIER.

4 Unless it's a special type of glass, like frosted or safety glass, a safe bet is to use 3 mm-thick glass for small windows, 4 mm for medium-sized ones and 6 mm for the biggest – ask your glass merchant if you're unsure. You'll also need a tub of putty and glazing sprigs.

5 Press a continuous strip of putty about 6 mm (¼ in) thick around the edges of the frame, pushing it in with your thumb.

JUST LIKE WOMEN, THIS STUFF IS PUTTY IN MY HANDS.

6 Position the pane of glass snugly into the putty. Start by resting the bottom edge on the bedding putty, then raise it to the vertical and press firmly all around the edge of the pane (never in the centre) to compress the putty to a thickness of about 3 mm (⅛ in). The excess will squeeze out on the inside, ready for trimming level with the inside of the frame. Next, tap in some glazing sprigs roughly 200 mm (8 in) apart all the way around the frame. They should lie flat against the glass and protrude slightly from the frame.

CAN YOU IMAGINE KEVIN DOING THIS ON HIS OWN? A HAMMER, A PANE OF GLASS ... IT'S OBVIOUS WHAT WOULD HAPPEN NEXT.

7 Press another thin strip of putty around the edge of the glass, covering the glazing sprigs, then use a putty knife to smooth it into a neat 45° angle.

GOODNESS! I DIDN'T THINK YOU'D MANAGE IT. YOU SEEM DIFFERENT SOMEHOW. WHAT ON EARTH'S GOING ON?

KEVIN! YOUR SUPPER IS READY!

CAROLINE'S NO FOOL. IT WON'T BE LONG BEFORE SHE GETS SUSPICIOUS ABOUT KEV'S REMARKABLE TRANSFORMATION.

CHANGING A PLUG...
WITHOUT BLOWING A FUSE

I'M SO EXCITED ABOUT MY NEW TOOLS, I CAN'T WAIT TO START FIXING EVERYTHING THAT'S BEEN BROKEN OR CHIPPED, BASHED OR TRASHED AROUND HERE.

CAPTAIN'S KIT

❋ flat-head and possibly cross-head screwdriver (depends on type of screws in plug) ❋ wire strippers or craft knife ❋ small electrical screwdriver for terminal screws ❋ new plug ❋ fuse of correct rating

BUT GOOD WORKMEN NEED FREQUENT TEA BREAKS, SO I SHOULD REPAIR THE DAMAGED PLUG ON THE KETTLE FIRST. WHERE'S THE TOOLBELT?

WOW

1 With his vast experience and cosmopolitan *je ne sais quoi*, the Captain is familiar with wiring systems all over the planet. To find out which you have, unscrew and remove the cover of the old plug, then check the diagrams (*right*). Loosen the terminal screws to slide the wires out of their terminals, or cut the flex if it's a factory-fitted plug.

WIRING DIAGRAMS

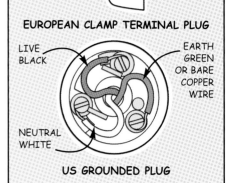

EARTH GREEN AND YELLOW

FUSE

NEUTRAL BLUE

LIVE BROWN

UK FUSED PLUG

EARTH GREEN AND YELLOW

LIVE BROWN

NEUTRAL BLUE

EUROPEAN CLAMP TERMINAL PLUG

LIVE BLACK

EARTH GREEN OR BARE COPPER WIRE

NEUTRAL WHITE

US GROUNDED PLUG

2 The new plug will usually come with a diagram showing how much wire needs to be bared and which bits connect where. Use wire strippers to bare the wires or, if you don't have any, a sharp craft knife will do the trick.

3 Now for the science bit! Some plugs need fuses. The fuse rating depends on the wattage of the appliance. Use a 3 amp fuse for those rated below 720 watts and a 13 amp fuse for between 720 and 3000 watts. You'll see where they go.

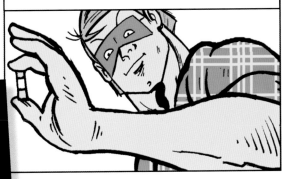

CAPTAIN'S TIP

Keep the live wire shortest so that if the plug is ripped off by accident, the live will break first.

4 Twist the filaments of each wire to make them neat, fold the tops down, then slide each wire into the correct terminal. They are generally held in place by clamping screws, which can be tightened with a cross-head or flat-head screwdriver. Alternatively, some plugs have a clamp terminal that you have to wind the twisted wire around clockwise. Secure the flex sheath in its clamp.

ALWAYS DOUBLE CHECK YOU'VE GOT THE WIRES IN THE RIGHT TERMINALS BEFORE PLUGGING IN. I SUSPECT THAT'S WHERE KEVIN WENT WRONG BEFORE.

YUP, THAT SEEMS TO BE OK.

5 Give your flex a little tug to check it's secure, then screw the plug back together again.

OH MAN, WITH ALL HIS DIY SHOPPING, IT LOOKS AS THOUGH KEVIN FORGOT TO BUY ANY TEA BAGS!

ELECTRICAL BASICS

RE-FUSING THAT SHORT CIRCUIT

FIRST THINGS FIRST

Find out where your main fusebox or consumer unit is located. There are different styles, but all of them have fuses designed to act as circuit breakers to protect the circuits in your house. If a circuit is overloaded, the fuse will trip and your electricity supply will cut out. You'll undoubtedly notice when this happens.

KNOW YOUR CIRCUITS

There will be separate circuits for the lighting on each floor of your home, and also for the electric sockets on each floor, while large appliances like cookers will have their own circuits as well. Get your electrician to test and label each of the circuits in your unit so it will be easier to track down the cause if anything blows in future.

WHAT TO DO IF YOU TRIP

Modern homes have a unit with miniature circuit breakers (MCBs) that trip off if anything goes wrong. There will be a main on/off switch in the unit and possibly a residual current device (RCD) on the circuits that are more at risk. If your electricity goes off, take a look at the unit to see if an MCB has tripped. If it has, switch off the main switch, try pushing the MCB in again, then switch on the mains. If the fault is still present, you won't be able to reset it – call an electrician.

Older homes have one (or sometimes more) fusebox with rewirable or cartridge fuses, as well as a main on/off switch. Some fuses have fuse wire wound around the terminals, which melts when the fuse blows. To fix this, switch off the main switch, remove the fuse holder, unfasten the terminal screws, take out the melted wire, replace it with new wire of the correct rating, making sure it's not too tight, then refix the screws.

Cartridge fuses either slip into spring clips or screw into position. Cartridge fuses are all different sizes, so ensure that you fit the correct one for your circuit.

BASIC ELECTRICAL TOOLKIT

So you're ready for any electrical emergency have these handy:

* A torch for when you're groping around in the dark. (And make sure the batteries are fresh!)
* Spare fuses, fuse wire or cartridges if you've got an old-fashioned kind of fusebox.
* Spare plug fuses and a small screwdriver for plug changing.
* Spare light bulbs!

ELECTRICAL NO-NOs

A STRETCH TOO FAR

Avoid over-stretching a flex to reach a socket. If your appliance flex is too short, ask an electrician to replace it for you, or to move the socket closer. Don't try this yourself.

CAUSING A PILE-UP

Don't overload your sockets with multiple adaptors stacked on top of each other. Buy a multi-way trailing socket with built-in surge control, or ask an electrician to add more sockets in your room, maybe by changing each single socket to a double one.

BE A BRIGHT SPARK

Turn off the light switch when replacing a blown light bulb. If you're not sure which way is off, you'll find out as soon as you insert the bulb!

GETTING IN A TWIST

Never let appliance cables get twisted or knotted, because the sheath could break and expose the wiring. If the sheath splits, don't try to patch it up with tape – replace the flex completely.

HEED THAT WARNING

Look out for warning signs that a socket might be damaged: scorch marks on the faceplate; sparks jumping when you plug in or unplug an appliance; the plug feeling warm; difficulty inserting a plug; or a cracked faceplate. Get your electrician to replace the socket entirely if you notice any of these.

DON'T BE WET

Remember that water and electricity don't mix. Don't ever use your hairdryer or any other electrical equipment in the bathroom. There's a reason why they don't put normal plug sockets in there!

REHANGING A DOOR...
WITHOUT ANY WHINGEING

CAPTAIN'S KIT
* screwdriver
* drill
* PVA wood glue
* dowel-jointing kit
* mallet * chisel
* pencil
* new hinges

I'D BETTER ASK THAT NICE OLD MAN IN THE DIY SHOP IF HE CAN GIVE ME SOME NEW HINGES. THESE LOOK A BIT KNACKERED.

MY DOOR FELL OFF AND THIS HINGE GOT MANGLED. CAN I HAVE ANOTHER?

OF COURSE. I'LL FIND SOME WITH LEAVES THE SAME SIZE AS THE OLD ONES SO YOU CAN USE THE SAME RECESSES. HAS THE WOOD SPLINTERED WHERE THE SCREWS CAME OUT?

ERM, I THINK SO. I DIDN'T REALLY LOOK.

IF SO, I SUGGEST YOU BUY A DOWEL-JOINTING KIT. YOU SIMPLY DRILL OUT THE EXISTING SCREW HOLES, PUSH IN SOME DOWELS AND THEN YOU HAVE A SECURE SURFACE TO INSERT THE NEW SCREWS INTO.

HMM. SOUNDS GOOD TO ME.

KEVIN WILL NEED TO MIND HIS TEMPER IN FUTURE – OR GET A PUNCHBAG INSTEAD OF TAKING HIS FRUSTRATIONS OUT ON HIS DOOR.

1 Throwing doors open violently puts a lot of strain on the fixing screws that hold the hinges in position and can tear them out of the screw holes, splintering the wood. If this has happened, you can't reuse the existing screw holes to replace your hinges because they'll be too big. Start by removing all the old screws to check the damage to the door and the door frame.

2 Hardwood dowel kits have several pieces of dowel, which tend to be about 9 mm (⅜ in) in diameter, along with matching drill bits. Fit the drill bit to your drill and use a piece of tape to mark a depth stop of 10–15 mm (⅜–⅝ in). Drill into each of the holes until you reach the depth stop.

3 Apply some PVA wood glue to each piece of dowel and push it into a hole.

> MOST HINGES HAVE THREE SCREWS PER LEAF, AND MOST DOORS HAVE TWO HINGES. IF YOU NEED TO DO THIS ON THE DOOR ITSELF AS WELL AS THE DOOR FRAME, YOU'LL NEED 12 BITS OF DOWEL. AS YOU CAN TELL, I'M AN ACE AT MENTAL ARITHMETIC.

4 Use a chisel to trim the pieces of dowel so that they are flush with the surface.

> REMEMBER THE GOLDEN RULE OF CHISELLING – DON'T REST YOUR HAND IN FRONT OF THE CHISEL BLADE.

> SCREW HOLES ARE NEVER IN THE SAME PLACE FROM ONE HINGE TO THE NEXT. IT'S ONE OF THOSE INTERESTING LITTLE FACTS OF LIFE.

5 Hold the new hinges over the old recesses and check that they fit, then poke a pencil or bradawl through the screw holes to mark the new screw positions.

CONTINUED OVER

THIS JOB HINGES ON FIXING YOUR SCREWS ACCURATELY, SO THERE'S EQUAL STRAIN ON EACH OF THEM.

6 Use a drill bit that's half the diameter of the screw shank to drill the pilot holes.

I WONDER WHY THEY'RE CALLED PILOT HOLES? S'POSE IT'S 'COS THEY SHOW THE SCREWS WHICH WAY TO GO.

8 Place the door in the open position in its frame and wedge it there with anything you have to hand. Professionals might use a triangular wedge of wood, but a couple of old screwdrivers or even some magazines would do the job.

7 Insert the screws through the hinges into the pilot holes in the door frame and tighten them until the hinge sits flush in its recess.

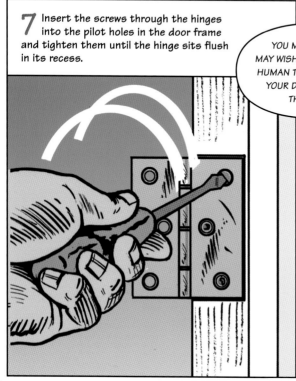

YOU MERE MORTALS MAY WISH TO GET ANOTHER HUMAN TO HELP YOU HOLD YOUR DOOR STEADY AT THIS STAGE.

9 Insert one screw through the top hinge into the door and another into the bottom. Test to see that it's moving freely, and that the latch is at the correct height to fit into its striking plate. (This should be fine if you're using the same size hinges that you had before and they're sitting in the same recesses.)

10 Make sure you tighten the screws evenly – no favouritism allowed.

FOR THE NEXT SPINE-CHILLING DOOR SAGA, SEE OVER THE PAGE...

3 Prop the door up securely, making sure it won't topple over while you're working on it.

IT ONLY NEEDS A LITTLE SHAVE DOWN HERE. IF IT WAS ANY MORE, I'D CUT IT WITH A SAW.

4 Avoid the area around the lock when planing the door edge. If it needs a lot taken off, you should plane the hinge side instead, because it is much easier to refit hinges than locks.

WHATEVER YOU DO, DON'T PLANE TOO MUCH. YOU CAN'T STICK WOOD SHAVINGS BACK ON AGAIN!

5 Use a medium-grade abrasive paper to sand down the planed edges.

6 Brush a wood primer over the newly exposed wood to seal and stop it absorbing moisture. You can then apply a coat of paint, or whatever finish you have on the rest of the door. Rehang it and check it moves freely now.

MMM, I DO LIKE A NICE FINISH.

THERE'S LOADS OF ADVICE ON PAINTING LATER (PAGES 136–49).

INDECENT EXPOSURE

HOW TO KEEP THAT DOOR SHUT!

Kevin's bathroom door won't latch properly, causing many an embarrassing moment as it slowly swings open while he's sitting on the toilet.

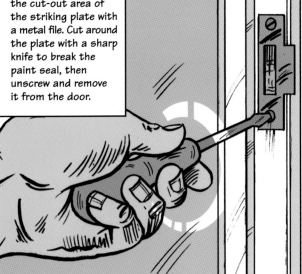

YIKES! MIND MY MODESTY!

Straight away the Captain sees that the latch is slightly too high for the striking plate. There are two ways he could deal with this.

HMMM. IT LOOKS AS THOUGH THIS LATCH NEEDS SOME HELP TO LATCH.

PLAN A

1 Sometimes it's possible to enlarge the cut-out area of the striking plate with a metal file. Cut around the plate with a sharp knife to break the paint seal, then unscrew and remove it from the door.

2 Hold the striking plate in a vice as you file away the excess metal, then refit it in your door using the original screws and screw holes.

THIS IS MUCH EASIER AND QUICKER THAN THE ALTERNATIVE METHOD, WHICH I'LL CALL PLAN B.

1 If the latch is more than a millimetre or so too high for the latch plate, there will be too much to file off. The other option is to remove the striking plate and move it to the right position for the latch. Fill the old screw holes with dowels, just as the Captain did on page 49. Cut them off flush with a sharp chisel.

2 Push the door closed and measure how high the latch bolt is relative to the striking plate. Mark this on the door frame to show how much higher the striking plate will have to be if it's going to spare Kev's blushes.

3 Use a hammer and chisel to enlarge the shallow recess in the door frame, so that the striking plate will sit just beyond the area that was marked with pencil. Cut across the grain first to outline the new larger recess, then slice along the grain to enlarge the recess, taking care not to overshoot. Depending on how much you're removing, you may also have to enlarge the deeper recess that the latch bolt fits in.

MAKE SURE YOUR CHISEL'S SUPER-SHARP OR IT COULD SPLINTER THE WOOD.

4 Hold your striking plate in position to mark the screw holes. Drill pilot holes in them (or use a bradawl), then reattach the plate to the door frame.

5 The door latches properly now, but it squeaks like something in a haunted house. The Captain gets a can of aerosol lubricant and squirts it into the hinges, making sure the oil doesn't drip on to the floor.

NO MORE EMBARRASSING TOILET PROBLEMS FOR OUR KEVIN. AT LEAST NOT THE DOOR KIND...

GETTING PLASTERED

I GUESS GREAT-AUNT HILDA WAS TOO HEAVY FOR A LITTLE PICTURE HOOK STUCK STRAIGHT INTO THE PLASTER. SHE FELL DOWN AND BROUGHT PART OF THE WALL WITH HER.

CAPTAIN'S KIT

FOR SMALL JOBS
* sponge
* all-purpose filler
* filling knife
* medium-grade abrasive paper and sanding block or orbital power sander
* paintbrush
* paint (or finish) to match the wall you're working on

EXTRAS FOR LARGER JOBS
* hammer and cold (masonry) chisel
* expanded metal mesh, if required

SPLOSH

1 Clean all the loose plaster debris from the hole – you can brush out the loose bits with a paintbrush. Dampen the surface, as this will help the filler adhere to the plaster. All-purpose filler comes ready-mixed or as a powder that needs to be mixed with water. Use a filling knife to spread it smoothly across the hole, making sure you work it in well.

JUST LIKE BUTTERING BREAD EXCEPT THE KNIFE IS SLIGHTLY BIGGER. AND THE BREAD'S NOT NORMALLY VERTICAL...

CAPTAIN'S TIP
Apply filler so that it stands out from the wall slightly. Once it has dried, you can sand it level.

2 Wait until the plaster is completely dry, then sand it smooth using a piece of medium-grade abrasive paper wrapped around a sanding block – or fitted to an orbital power sander.

GOOD JOB KEVIN KEPT SOME LEFTOVER PAINT FROM THE LAST TIME HE PAINTED THIS ROOM – IT WOULD BE HARD TO FIND A BLUE THAT'S QUITE AS BLUE AS THIS AGAIN.

If your cracks are less than 6 mm (¼ in) wide, they can be filled with one layer of all-purpose filler.

1 If you've got very large cracks and holes, they'll require special treatment. Before adding any filler, chip away all the loose and damaged plaster with a hammer and chisel, then undercut the edges of the hole with a craft knife.

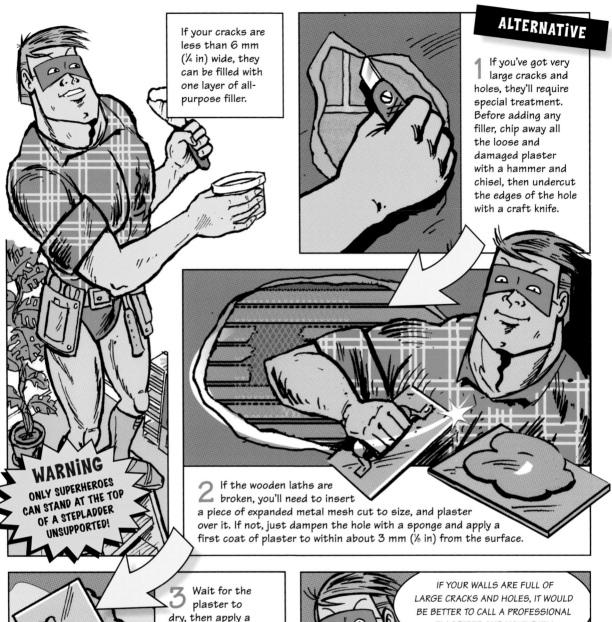

2 If the wooden laths are broken, you'll need to insert a piece of expanded metal mesh cut to size, and plaster over it. If not, just dampen the hole with a sponge and apply a first coat of plaster to within about 3 mm (⅛ in) from the surface.

WARNING
ONLY SUPERHEROES CAN STAND AT THE TOP OF A STEPLADDER UNSUPPORTED!

3 Wait for the plaster to dry, then apply a second coat. Use a decorator's float to level it with the surrounding wall – but make sure you ask the decorator's permission first! Once it is completely dry, sand it smooth and repaint.

IF YOUR WALLS ARE FULL OF LARGE CRACKS AND HOLES, IT WOULD BE BETTER TO CALL A PROFESSIONAL PLASTERER AND HAVE THEM RESURFACED.

HANGING PICTURES...
WITHOUT KNOCKING DOWN WALLS

CAPTAIN'S KIT
* pipe and cable detector
* 2 mirror plates with 38-mm (1½-in) screws   * pencil
* bradawl
* flat-head screwdriver
* spirit level   * safety goggles
* drill and bit (depending on wall type)   * masking tape
* wallplugs

1 Some walls are solid masonry, while others are plasterboard or lath-and-plaster within a frame of wooden studs. You should be able to tell the difference by tapping the wall with your knuckle and listening for a solid or a hollow sound. If you're hanging heavy weights on a stud wall, the fixings should be attached to the wooden studs.

CAPTAIN'S TIP
A single-pin picture hook will support a glazed picture up to about 900 x 600 mm (3 x 2 ft). A double-pin hook will support one about half as big again. If you're hanging a mirror or a picture in a heavy, ornate frame (like Great Aunt Hilda's), you'll need mirror plates.

2 Use a pipe and cable detector before choosing your fixing positions. Never drill above or below light switches or electric sockets because the supply cables often run vertically up or down to them. You can also use this nifty gadget to find the studs in a plaster-board wall, as it will detect the nails in the studs.

3 Great Aunt Hilda's weight will need two mirror plates on the top of the frame to support it. Position them equidistant from the sides. Check they're straight, make small holes with a bradawl through the screw holes, then screw the mirror plates into the frame.

THIS PICTURE SURE IS HEAVY. IF IT WASN'T FOR MY SUPERB CAPTAIN COMPETENT MUSCLES, I'D NEED TO GET AN ASSISTANT TO HOLD IT WHILE I SCREWED IT TO THE WALL.

4 Use a long spirit level to check your fixing holes are level.

CAN'T HAVE YOU ALL CROOKED NOW, CAN WE? YOU LITTLE MINX!

IT'S A GOOD IDEA TO TAPE AN ENVELOPE ON THE WALL BELOW TO CATCH THE DRILL DUST. SAVES LOADS OF VACUUMING LATER!

5 If your picture is going on a solid wall, choose a masonry drill bit. If you're drilling into a stud, choose a twist bit. Mark a depth stop on your drill with masking tape (see page 29). Drill holes in the positions you've marked and tap a plug into each.

6 Insert your screws through the mirror plates and into the plugs. Screw them in.

CAPTAIN'S TIP
If you don't want to position your picture where there are studs, see page 17 for some tips on hollow-wall fixings.

MORE NiFTY WAYS OF HANGING ON WALLS

I'LL NEED ONE FOR MY RAINCOAT, ONE FOR MY DUFFEL COAT AND ONE FOR MY ANORAK.

1 Kevin wants to put up coat hooks, but it's a solid masonry wall. He'll need a hammer-action drill and long screws and plugs. Time for Captain Competent to take over...

USE SCREWS THAT ARE LONG ENOUGH TO EXTEND 25 MM (1 IN) INTO THE MASONRY, OR YOUR COATS WILL FALL DOWN IN A TRICE!

PIECE OF CAKE!

2 Mark the spot, drill the holes, insert your plugs and screw in your coat hooks. What could be simpler, folks?

CAPTAIN'S TIP
Start the hole first before you turn the hammer action on. This will stop the bit slipping off target.

iN THE KiTCHEN

3 Now you've caught the hanging habit, how do you fancy putting some hooks for tea towels in the kitchen? These aren't heavy, so a screw or a hook with a threaded shank will suffice.

4 In wood, you can just screw your hooks right in. If it's a masonry wall, you'll need to drill holes for wallplugs.

60

SWIVEL

5 Insert a plug, then screw in the tea-towel hook.

I GUESS THIS MEANS THERE'S NO EXCUSE FOR NOT WASHING THE DISHES NOW... EXCEPT I'VE JUST THOUGHT OF ANOTHER IMPORTANT HANGING TASK TO BE DONE!

SAFETY

USE THAT PIPE AND CABLE DETECTOR EVERY TIME YOU DRILL, TO AVOID FLOODING OR ELECTROCUTION — OR BOTH!

IN THE BEDROOM

6 The Captain decides to hang a picture of Caroline by Kevin's bed. It's very light, so there's no need to find a stud. A tiny picture hook with a slim masonry pin will take care of it.

THAT'LL MAKE UP FOR HIM FORGETTING HER BIRTHDAY...

PICTURE HOOKS COME IN ONE- OR TWO-PIN FORM.

7 There's a string across the back of the frame, so he just needs to hammer a nail through the hole in the picture hook, then slip it on.

PHEW, I'VE SAVED THE WORLD FROM ANOTHER HANGING DISASTER – TIME TO RELAX.

LET'S GET THIS STRAIGHT
SOME SHELF FIXES

CAPTAIN'S KIT
* spirit level
* screwdriver
* all-purpose filler
* filling knife
* paint to match wall
* abrasive paper and sanding block
* pencil * drill and bit
* screws and plugs
* brackets

EITHER THAT SHELF IS SQUINT OR IT'S TIME I GOT SOME NEW GLASSES. LOOKS LIKE ANOTHER JOB FOR CAPTAIN COMPETENT!

DOO DOO-DOO! CAPTAIN COMPETENT TO THE RESCUE!

1 The Captain uses a spirit level to confirm his hunch. The shelf's as crooked as a politician.

THE BUBBLE NEVER LIES.

2 This one's so squint that there's nothing for it but to unscrew the brackets, take the shelf off the wall and start again. Fill the old screw holes with filler, sand them down and paint them before you put the shelf back up. When you're marking the new shelf fixing points, use your spirit level to check they're level.

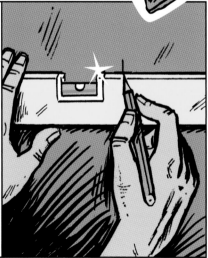

3 You know the procedure for attaching things to walls now. Check for pipes and cables before you drill. Make your holes, push in the plugs, then attach your brackets with their screws.

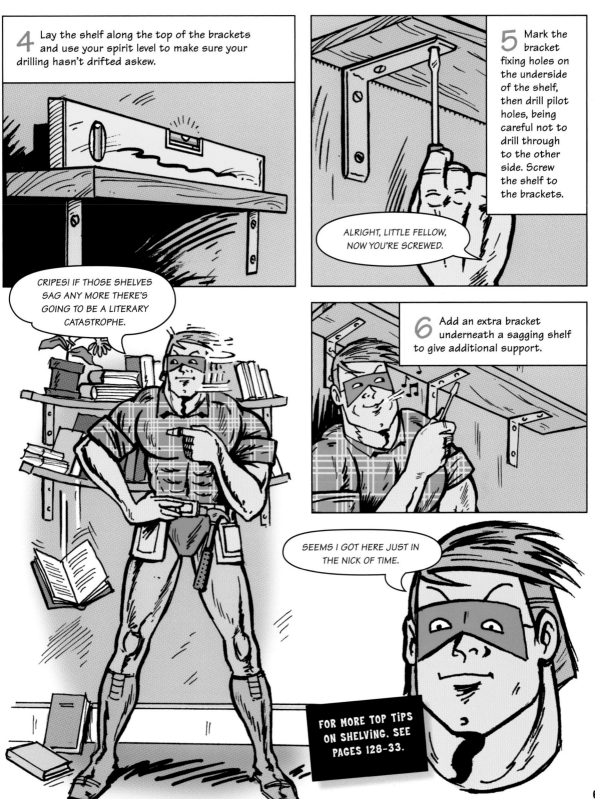

4 Lay the shelf along the top of the brackets and use your spirit level to make sure your drilling hasn't drifted askew.

5 Mark the bracket fixing holes on the underside of the shelf, then drill pilot holes, being careful not to drill through to the other side. Screw the shelf to the brackets.

ALRIGHT, LITTLE FELLOW, NOW YOU'RE SCREWED.

CRIPES! IF THOSE SHELVES SAG ANY MORE THERE'S GOING TO BE A LITERARY CATASTROPHE.

6 Add an extra bracket underneath a sagging shelf to give additional support.

SEEMS I GOT HERE JUST IN THE NICK OF TIME.

FOR MORE TOP TIPS ON SHELVING, SEE PAGES 128-33.

THE TROUBLE WITH DRAWERS
AN OPEN AND SHUT CASE

IT'S FUNNY, I NEVER REALLY NOTICED UNTIL NOW, BUT THINGS ARE A BIT AWRY IN MY KITCHEN.

CAPTAIN'S KIT
* PVA adhesive * chisel
* flat-head and cross-head screwdrivers
* abrasive paper and sanding block
* new runners (if required)
* screws (if required)
* dowels cut to size

DRAWERS GET PRETTY ROUGH TREATMENT, SO IT'S NO WONDER THEY MISBEHAVE FROM TIME TO TIME.

1 If a drawer flies out of its hole, it's probably because the drawer stop is broken. If you can find it and it's intact, glue it back on again. If not, make a new one from an offcut of wood.

2 Drawers will stick if the runners are worn or broken. Unscrew and remove them then scrape off any old glue with a chisel blade.

IF A RUNNER IS BADLY WORN, YOU MAY HAVE TO REPLACE IT.

3 To refit a runner, apply PVA adhesive to the back, then screw it into place using countersunk screws that are big enough to grip the screw holes.

CARAMBA! I'M BEING ATTACKED BY A FLYING COLANDER!

4 To realign a wonky cupboard door, use a cross-head screwdriver to adjust the screws in the hinges that hold the door to the frame. Loosen the larger screw of each hinge to move the door in or out, then tighten it again. Adjust the smaller screw to move the door from side to side as well as helping it to open and close properly. It's remarkably easy.

> MAKE SURE YOU ADJUST THE TOP AND BOTTOM ONES EQUALLY, SO THEY DON'T GET UNHINGED!

5 There are oodles of invisible fixings that can be used to attach drawer fronts to drawers. If your units came as part of a flatpack, you may be able to buy replacement retaining clips (*see pages 172–3 for all the flatpack know-how you'll need*).

> DOUBLE BUBBLE DOWEL TROUBLE.

6 Kevin's wooden drawers are held together with glued-in dowels. To repair them, the Captain must first clean off any old dried glue, then squirt a little PVA adhesive into the holes before reinserting the dowels that hold the front in place. He also applies PVA down the sides of the drawer front, then ties a strap around the drawer to hold the front in place until it dries.

7 Unfortunately, the Captain doesn't clean the glue from his fingers before answering the telephone.

> OOH, YUCK! JUST MY LUCK!

CAPTAIN'S TIP
Whenever you're glueing, make sure you have the appropriate solvent close at hand.

A CURTAIN RAISER

OH MAN, I'VE BEEN MEANING TO FIX MY MOTHER'S CURTAIN TRACK UP AGAIN FOR AGES.

HONESTLY, KEVIN, JUST LEAVE IT. I'LL GET A HANDYMAN AROUND SOON. WE DON'T WANT YOU HAVING AN ACCIDENT NOW, DO WE?

HMMM, THIS SOUNDS LIKE A JOB FOR CAPTAIN COMPETENT.

CAPTAIN'S KIT

* tape measure
* pencil
* spirit level
* curtain track kit
* pipe and cable detector
* drill and bit
* screws and plugs

1 The curtain rail should be the width of the window plus another 150 mm (6 in) on each side. Draw a pencil guideline running about 150 mm (6 in) above the top of the window and use a spirit level to check that it's horizontal. If it's closer to the ceiling, measure down from that instead (although first check that your ceiling is horizontal). Extend your guideline beyond the edge of the window to suit the length of the rail, then measure 250 mm (10 in) in from each end and make a pencil cross; this is where your end brackets will go. Space your other fixing positions at equal intervals along the rail.

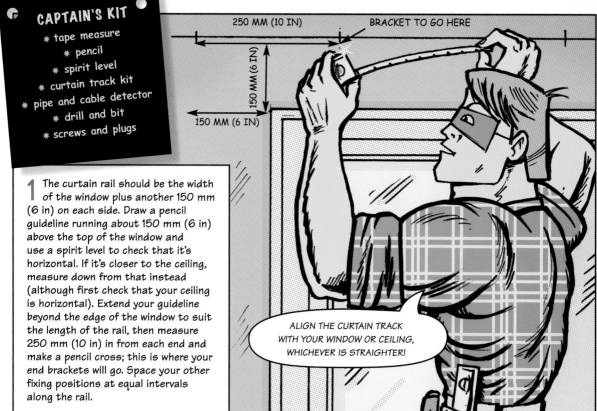

250 MM (10 IN)

BRACKET TO GO HERE

150 MM (6 IN)

150 MM (6 IN)

ALIGN THE CURTAIN TRACK WITH YOUR WINDOW OR CEILING, WHICHEVER IS STRAIGHTER!

2 The big problem with putting up curtain tracks is getting a firm fixing in the wall above the window. Until you start working, you can't tell what might be up there beneath the plaster – a wooden beam, or a steel or concrete lintel. Check with a pipe and cable detector, then drill a test hole to find out. Choose your drill bit accordingly (see page 13).

I'M USING LONG SCREWS THAT WILL EXTEND ABOUT 38 MM (1½ IN) INTO THE WALL. KEVIN'S WERE FAR TOO SHORT AND JUST FELL OUT AGAIN.

3 Follow the instructions on your curtain track kit because there are different ways of assembling them. Normally, you screw the mounting clips into position, making sure the track slots face forwards.

YOUR KIT MIGHT BE SLIGHTLY DIFFERENT FROM MINE, BUT THE PRINCIPLE WILL BE THE SAME.

4 Fit the sliders on to the track, then clip it into place and insert the end stops.

DON'T FORGET THOSE END STOPS OR YOUR CURTAINS WILL SLIDE RIGHT OFF.

YEE-UCH! WE SUPERHEROES CAN FIX EVERYTHING EXCEPT BAD TASTE.

ALTERNATiVELY

If Kevin's mother had wanted a curtain pole instead of a track, the technique for putting it up would be similar, but the brackets are often attached to plastic fixing bosses secured with plugs and screws.

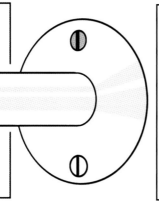

In this case, you would slide the pole on to the bracket, screw it into place following the instructions on the pack, put on the curtain rings and screw on the finials (the fancy bits at the ends). Easy-peasy.

BLINDINGLY OBVIOUS!

CAPTAIN'S KIT
* bradawl
* cross-head screwdriver
* roller blind kit
* hacksaw (if required)
* scissors (if required)
* pipe and cable detector
* drill and bit

GOODNESS, WHAT'S HAPPENED TO YOU? HAVE YOU DONE A COURSE, OR HAD A BRAIN TRANSPLANT? WHERE'S MY CLUMSY SON GONE?

I DON'T SUPPOSE YOU COULD FIT THIS ROLLER BLIND OVER THE WINDOW FOR ME? THE NOSY PARKERS NEXT DOOR KEEP PEERING IN TO SEE WHAT I'M COOKING.

OK, MA, NO PROBLEM AT ALL.

CAN I WATCH MY BIG CLEVER SON AT WORK?

SHE'D BE AMAZED IF SHE KNEW ABOUT KEVIN'S SECRET WEAPON... ME!

NO, SORRY MA. I GET NERVOUS IF THERE'S AN AUDIENCE.

1 The Captain holds the blind in place and uses a bradawl to mark the fixing positions for the brackets. He's going to screw them directly into the wooden window frame. If you are fixing them to a masonry or hollow wall, you'll need the appropriate drill bits, screws and plugs. With uPVC windows, you'll have to drill pilot holes and use self-tapping screws to fix the brackets into the frames (ask for these in your DIY shop).

CAPTAIN'S TIP
If you can't find a blind that fits the dimensions of your window, buy the next size up and cut the pole with a small hacksaw. Trim the fabric with a straightedge and a sharp knife.

POSITION THE BLIND'S CONTROL PANEL ON THE SIDE YOU WANT TO OPERATE IT FROM. MA IS RIGHT-HANDED, SO I'LL PUT HERS ON THE RIGHT.

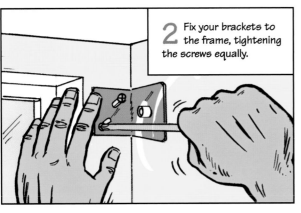

2 Fix your brackets to the frame, tightening the screws equally.

CRIPES, HERE SHE COMES! I NEED TO GET THE BELT OFF QUICK!

TARNATION! SMASHING THAT TILE WASN'T PART OF THE PLAN.

I JUST WONDERED IF YOU'D LIKE A GLASS OF LEMONADE, SON?

PHEW! THAT WAS CLOSE, HOPE SHE DOESN'T SPOT THAT TILE!

BACK TO THE PLOT

3 Follow the instructions on your roller blind kit to assemble the blind. Mount it on its brackets, then raise and lower it using the control cords. Congratulate yourself on a job well done – unless, like Kevin, you cracked a tile in the process...

HEEEY! I'M ON A ROLL! BETTER SORT OUT THAT TILE.

CRACKING UP
Try not to break any tiles while you work, but if the worst comes to the worst, turn the page for advice on tile traumas.

GET CRACKING...
AND FIX THAT BROKEN TILE

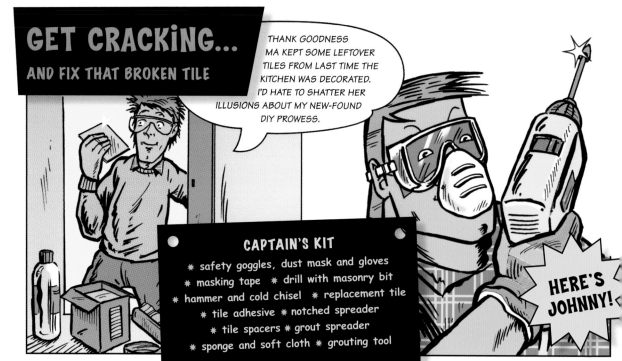

THANK GOODNESS MA KEPT SOME LEFTOVER TILES FROM LAST TIME THE KITCHEN WAS DECORATED. I'D HATE TO SHATTER HER ILLUSIONS ABOUT MY NEW-FOUND DIY PROWESS.

HERE'S JOHNNY!

CAPTAIN'S KIT
* safety goggles, dust mask and gloves
* masking tape * drill with masonry bit
* hammer and cold chisel * replacement tile
* tile adhesive * notched spreader
* tile spacers * grout spreader
* sponge and soft cloth * grouting tool

1 This can get a bit messy — and dangerous. You need to scrape the grout from around the damaged tile, then drill some holes in it so that you can chisel it off. Shards will fly off in all directions, so make sure you wear full safety gear. You can buy a special ceramic tile drill bit, or just use a masonry bit at slow speed. Easy does it, tiger.

CAPTAIN'S TIP
Put masking tape on the edges of the surrounding tiles to protect them. If you find the drill bit slipping on the tile surface, make an X shape with masking tape and drill through that.

2 Cut away the broken bits of tile using a hammer and cold chisel, and chip away as much of the underlying adhesive as you can, so that the replacement tile will sit flush with the surrounding surface.

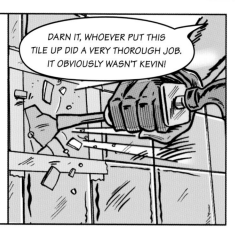

DARN IT, WHOEVER PUT THIS TILE UP DID A VERY THOROUGH JOB. IT OBVIOUSLY WASN'T KEVIN!

3 Spread tile adhesive on the back of the new tile, using a notched spreader to produce a groovy effect.

4 Press the tile into place, fitting tile spacers underneath it to stop it sliding down while the adhesive dries and to leave space for grout to be applied later...

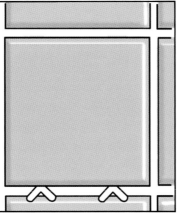

YUCK, MY LEAST FAVOURITE PART OF THE JOB – BUT SUPERHERO WORKMEN ALWAYS TIDY UP AS THEY GO ALONG.

5 Wait until the adhesive has dried – check the pack for drying times – then use a grout spreader to press grout into the joints.

I ALWAYS GROUT DIAGONALLY ACROSS A TILE TO GET IT INTO THE JOINTS.

6 Wipe the grout off the tile surface before it sets hard. It's much easier that way – believe me!

7 For a truly professional finish, run a grouting tool along the joints to neaten them up, before removing any masking tape and giving your tiles a final polish with a soft cloth.

TWINKLE, TWINKLE LITTLE TILE...

WANT TO GET MORE AMBITIOUS WITH YOUR TILING? SEE PAGES 160–9.

BURGLAR-PROOFING YOUR HOME

I'VE JUST HEARD ON THE NEWS THAT LOTS OF HOMES AROUND HERE HAVE BEEN BURGLED. WHAT IF THEY COME AND TRY MINE?

NOT TO WORRY, MA. I'LL HAVE A CHECK AROUND TO SEE HOW SECURE THE HOUSE IS.... ERM, DO YOU ALWAYS LEAVE THE KEY IN THE LOCK LIKE THAT, JUST UNDER A GLASS PANEL? IT'S MAYBE NOT THE BEST IDEA.

I SEE NONE OF YOUR WINDOWS HAS LOCKS. WE CAN FIX THAT IN A JIFFY.

YOU'VE GOT A GOOD SOLID FRONT DOOR, BUT IT WOULD BE BETTER IF YOU COULD SEE WHO THE CALLER IS BEFORE YOU OPEN IT. I THINK I'LL JUST GO ON A SHOPPING TRIP. CATCH YOU LATER!

SHE'S GETTING ON A BIT – 60 YEARS OLD AND SHE LIVES ON HER OWN...

WHAT DO YOU MEAN OLD? AT 60, SHE'S STILL A SPRING CHICKEN!

1 Fitting a mortise lock is a tricky job if you're not a superhero because you have to cut out a recess of exactly the right size in the centre of the door's width. If your chisel slips, it'll be time to get a new door. You might find it easier to take the door off its hinges so you're not working sideways!

2 Position the lock about a third of the way up your door. Measure and mark a line in pencil right in the centre of the door's width, then mark the top, bottom and sides of the lock's shape, making sure it is dead centre.

PYTHAGORAS, EAT YOUR HEART OUT!

3 Mark a flat drill bit with a depth stop that is exactly the same as the depth of the lock's casing. Very carefully bore a line of holes along the central line in your rectangle.

4 Using a sharp chisel and a hammer, pare out the wood to create the rectangular shapes for the lock's casing and face plate, and the shallow recess that will take the fore-end of the lock. Try the lock in place to see if it fits, then adjust if necessary.

CHISEL CAREFULLY! REMEMBER YOU CAN ALWAYS TAKE MORE WOOD OUT, BUT YOU CAN'T PUT IT BACK IN AGAIN!

5 Holding the lock casing in position on the outside or inside of the door, at the correct height, push a pencil or bradawl through to mark the position of the keyhole.

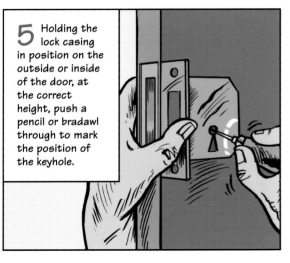

6 Drill holes for the keyhole then cut it to the exact shape with a padsaw. Cut the slot with a padsaw and chisel.

FOR A BACK DOOR, YOU ONLY NEED TO CUT A KEYHOLE ON THE INSIDE. FOR THE MAIN DOOR, USUALLY AT THE FRONT, YOU'LL NEED TO CUT A KEYHOLE FROM BOTH SIDES SO YOU CAN GET IN FROM THE OUTSIDE AS WELL AS OUT FROM THE INSIDE!

7 Screw your lock into place and try it out. Then screw a key plate over the keyhole (or keyholes).

I SPECIALIZE IN KEYHOLE SURGERY.

8 Remember on pages 54–5 when we fixed Kevin's bathroom door by moving the striking plate? Follow these instructions to position the striking plate for your brand-new mortise lock.

NEVER LEAVE YOUR KEY IN THE LOCK. YOU MIGHT AS WELL PAINT A HUGE SIGN FOR BURGLARS SAYING, 'HEY, GUYS! HELP YOURSELVES!'

WiNDOWS WiTH ATTiTUDE...

BURGLARS WON'T MESS WITH THEM

1 With casement windows, you need to fit the body of the locking catches to the window frames and attach lockplates to the windows. On this window, the Captain decides to fit two locks, top and bottom, to the large hinged panel and one on the smaller hinged panel.

2 Close the window completely and lock the two parts of your window lock together. Hold the body of the window lock against the fixed frame and the lockplate against the opening frame in the position you have chosen. Draw around them both in pencil, and mark the screw positions with a bradawl.

> FIT WINDOW LOCKS ON ANY WINDOWS THAT WILL OPEN WIDE ENOUGH TO ADMIT A SKINNY INTRUDER.

3 Separate the lockplate from the body of the lock and screw it in place on the casement. The correct size screws should be supplied with the lock.

4 Drill pilot holes into the edge of the fixed frame to take the body of the lock.

5 Lock the body to the lockplate you have already attached, then screw the body into the pilot holes you made in the frame. Simple as that!

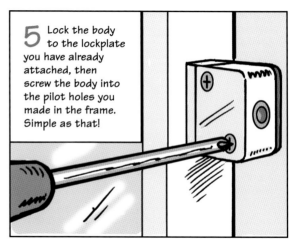

6 If you have window stays with holes in them, you can attach a locking device that will hold the window in a closed or open position. On metal-framed windows, this may be the only way you can fit a lock.

> KEEP THE KEYS TO THE WINDOW LOCKS HIDDEN NEARBY IN CASE YOU NEED TO ESCAPE QUICKLY IN THE EVENT OF FIRE.

ALTERNATIVELY

Locking devices on sash windows need to clamp together the two rails in the middle (called meeting rails). One of the simplest types of device to fit is the dual screw. As the name suggests, a part is inserted into each rail then they're screwed together.

1 Make sure your windows are closed and the meeting rails aligned. Choose a drill bit to match the screw size and mark a depth stop that is the width of the inner rail plus the length of the outer barrel of the locking screw. Drill through the inner rail and into the outer one.

> IT'S BEST TO FIT DUAL SCREWS IN PAIRS AT EACH SIDE OF A MEETING RAIL.

2 Screw the longer barrel into the inner rail, then push the bottom sash up and pull the top one all the way down so that you can insert the shorter barrel into the hole in the outer rail.

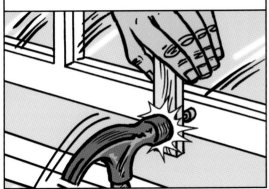

3 Close the sashes together again and screw the two pieces together with the key to lock your window.

> THERE ARE DIFFERENT KINDS OF WINDOW LOCK, BUT MOST FOLLOW THE SAME PRINCIPLES. IF ALL ELSE FAILS, READ THE MANUFACTURER'S INSTRUCTIONS!

NOW FOR THE REALLY EASY BiTS...

SPYGLASSES, CHAINS AND SMOKE ALARMS

THE INSTRUCTIONS SAY TO INSTALL THIS SPY GLASS AT THE CORRECT HEIGHT FOR YOUR EYE, BUT I THINK KEVIN'S MOTHER'S A BIT SHORTER THAN ME – ALL HUMANS ARE.

1 Draw around the spyglass, then use a flat drill bit (usually 12 mm/½ in size) to drill a hole that's the correct size through the door until the bit just penetrates the other side. Complete the hole by drilling from the other side – this way you'll have a clean cut on each side.

2 Insert the threaded piece of the spyglass from the outside and the collar from the inside, then just screw them together.

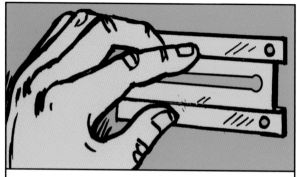

3 To fit a door chain, screw the slotted plate to the door at the height you have chosen, using screws that are at least 30 mm (1¼ in) long.

4 Chisel out a recess in the door frame where the chain will be attached. Select a position that will allow you to see out, but won't let anyone on the outside get their hand in to unfasten it. Screw it into place.

DON'T FORGET TO USE YOUR CHAIN WHENEVER DEALING WITH CALLERS YOU DON'T KNOW – EVEN THE SUPERHERO VARIETY.

5 Position smoke alarms in hallways on each floor of your house. Keep them at least 300 mm (1 ft) away from any light fittings and the wall/ceiling angle.

MAKE SURE THE BATTERIES ARE WORKING IN YOUR SMOKE ALARMS, OR THEIR ONLY VALUE WILL BE DECORATIVE.

SOUNDS LIKE SOMEONE'S BURNED THE TOAST.

GOOD GRIEF, KEVIN. IS THAT SOME NEW LP YOU'VE BOUGHT?

AHA! IT SEEMS YOUR SMOKE ALARM IS IN GOOD WORKING ORDER.

BY THE WAY, THERE'S A HOLE IN THE KITCHEN LINO. I WAS MEANING TO MENTION IT.

SEE PAGE 202 FOR ADVICE ON LAYING NEW LINO.

CAPTAIN COMPETENT'S

PLUMBING

Now you've mastered the easy fixes, it's time to head into the bathroom for some slightly (but only very slightly) more complex work. If, like Kevin, you're daunted by the prospect of replacing the washer on a tap, the Captain will wipe out any fears with a wave of his spanner. In this inspirational lesson, you'll learn all the superhero plumbing basics from finding your stopcock to clearing an S-bend. No more water worries!

HELP, I'M GOING TO NEED THAT MAGIC TOOLBELT AGAIN – AND FLUFFY'S NONE TOO PLEASED WITH HER WET FUR.

BEFORE YOU START MESSING WITH WATER, YOU'LL NEED TO KNOW A FEW ESSENTIAL FACTS...

LEAKS, FLOODS AND OTHER PLUMBING EMERGENCIES

STIFF STOPCOCKS

There is a main stopcock at the point where the water pipe from your local water supplier enters your house. Quite often you will find this stopcock under the kitchen sink. It's worth finding out where yours is and checking that you can turn it easily. If it has stiffened up, apply a little penetrating oil to loosen it so you're not caught out in an emergency.

FEELING DRAINED

If you ever need to work on part of your plumbing system, you will have to drain the whole system or at least the part you are working on – or you're going to get pretty wet! To drain the system, turn off the main stopcock and run all the taps. If you're just working on one fitting, like a sink or a toilet, you may find an isolating valve underneath that can shut off the water supply to them. If it is a tap fed from a storage tank or hot water system, you may need to drain the tank.

FLOOD ALERT!

So what should you do if you are wakened up at night by water cascading through your bedroom ceiling on to your Spiderman duvet?

First of all, turn off the electricity at your consumer unit <u>without delay</u>. Always keep a torch handy for this kind of eventuality. Next, turn off the water at the main stopcock. And thirdly, call an emergency plumber. Water storage tanks in lofts can contain a lot of water, which could cause the ceiling to collapse, so don't go back into your bedroom if the water is still pouring through. Follow the procedure to drain the system, running all taps. Don't turn the electricity back on again until you've had any sockets and cables that were exposed to water checked out by an electrician.

ACCIDENTAL FOUNTAINS

What should Kevin have done when he not so cleverly hit that water pipe while nailing down a floorboard in the hall?

The easiest thing would have been to leave the nail in place and phone a plumber. Alternatively, if he'd had a pipe repair clamp in the house, he could have shut off the water to that pipe and screwed the clamp around the damaged section for a watertight temporary repair. We're not going to get into cutting and joining new sections of pipe in this book – gotta let the plumbers earn a living.

AN ICE PROBLEM

what should you do about frozen pipes?

This is one of the most common plumbing problems in winter, causing blockages and even making pipes burst. It's best to avoid the problem altogether by lagging any cold-water pipes that run through unheated areas of the house. You can buy pre-slit foam-backed tubing that is sealed in place with adhesive tape. If you do get a frozen pipe, thaw it by applying cloths soaked in boiling water, or a hot water bottle, or by playing a hairdryer over the affected area. But NEVER use a blowtorch to try and defrost a pipe. Don't even think about it.

NO WATER

You fancy a hot bath, and you've got your ducks and bubbles all lined up, but when you turn on the tap - nothing happens. What can you do?

Well, first of all try the kitchen sink cold tap. If there's no water coming from it, then check that your stopcock hasn't been turned off. If the stopcock is on and there's still no water, call the local water authority because it looks as though it's their fault. If the kitchen taps are working, you'll have to take a look at your cold water cistern (probably in the loft).

Is the cistern empty? Is the ball valve stuck? Jiggle your ball up and down a bit. If there's no flow of water when your valve is held open, you've maybe got ice in your rising main and it's plumber time! Alternatively, if the cistern is full, then there must be a blockage in a hot water or cold water supply pipe somewhere between here and the bath taps. What a drag! Call the plumber, then go share a bath with a close friend.

WARM UP YOUR PIPE WITH A BLAST OF WARN AIR. DON'T JUST CONCENTRATE ON THE ONE AREA, THOUGH. KEEP MOVING AROUND.

THE TOP 3 PLUMBER'S SECRET WEAPONS

PTFE TAPE

(short for polytetrafluoroethylene, if you must know) is essential for sealing threaded connections in taps and so forth. Just wrap it three times around the threads for a watertight seal.

FLEXIBLE SILICONE SEALANT

does exactly what it says - gives a flexible waterproof seal around bathroom fittings. It's easy to use as well: cut the nozzle off at a 45° angle and squeeze the tube, like toothpaste! Except not on to your toothbrush, obviously.

CRANKED SPANNERS

are great for loosening nuts in awkward places, like the nuts that are found on radiator valves. You'll find that you're struggling to do plumbing repairs without a couple.

UNBLOCKING THE SINK

IN WHICH CAROLINE SENDS KEVIN AROUND THE BEND...

I DON'T KNOW WHAT TO DO. MY KITCHEN SINK IS COMPLETELY BLOCKED, BUT I CAN'T GET A PLUMBER AROUND TODAY BECAUSE I HAVE TO GO TO WORK.

YOU DON'T NEED A PLUMBER, PUMPKIN. LEAVE IT TO ME AND I'LL HAVE IT ALL SORTED BY THE TIME YOU GET HOME.

CAPTAIN'S KIT
* sink plunger
* rubber gloves
* bucket
* wire coathanger
* drain auger, if required

1 Captain Competent gets on the case. Straightforward sink blockages can be cleared with a sink plunger. Place it over the plughole, press a damp cloth over the sink overflow opening and plunge up and down for a few minutes. Get a nice bouncy rhythm going!

UH-OH. LOOKS AS THOUGH THERE'S SOMETHING NASTY CAUGHT IN THE TRAP UNDERNEATH THE SINK.

2 Traps under sinks often get blocked with accumulated grease, food scraps, hair and general gunk. You should be able to unscrew yours fairly easily...

FLUSHED WITH SUCCESS

THIS IS A DIRECT-ACTION WC, WHICH IS A PRETTY SIMPLE SYSTEM. IT'LL BE MORE AWKWARD IF YOU HAVE A CLOSE-COUPLED WC WHERE THE CISTERN SITS DIRECTLY ON THE PAN

CAPTAIN'S KIT
* wooden batten * string
* pipe wrench * bucket
* new flap valve, if required
* siphon, if required
* screwdriver * pliers
* wire wool or abrasive paper, if required * scissors, if required
* new ball valve washer, if required

2 Next, check that your flush handle connects up like this one. There should be a wire link from the handle to a lever that lifts a plate at the bottom of the siphon chamber. As the plate rises, the flap valve operates and water is pushed up the chamber and down the flush pipe. If the wire link is loose, tighten it or replace it with thick wire. If it's OK, and the flush mechanism is not working, chances are you've got a dodgy flap valve.

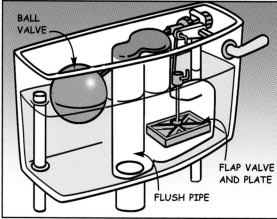

BALL VALVE

FLAP VALVE AND PLATE

FLUSH PIPE

1 Kevin re-calls Captain Competent to duty, and he knows just what to do. First of all, check the water level in your cistern. It should be about 25 mm (1 in) below the overflow outlet. If it's too low, or too high, you need to adjust your ball valve (see page 88). Caroline's water level is fine, though. Good-oh.

3 Before replacing the flap valve, the Captain needs to empty Caroline's cistern. He places a wooden batten across the cistern and ties the ball valve arm to it with a piece of string (this will stop the cistern refilling when the water level drops). If your flush still works and you can flush the water out of your cistern, do so. The Captain can't, because Caroline's flush is broken, so he'll have to siphon the water out.

THIS IS PRETTY EASY, SO DON'T GET IN A FLAP ABOUT IT. HA, HA!

4 Use a large pipe wrench to undo the nut beneath the cistern that holds the flush pipe in place. Disconnect it and push it to one side. (This only applies to washdown cisterns. For close-coupled ones, you'll find screw fittings attaching the overflow pipe and water supply pipe to the cistern.)

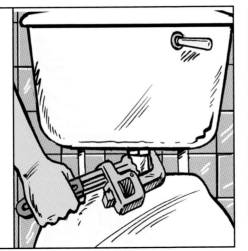

5 Disconnect the nut that holds the siphon to the inside of the cistern. Some water will flow out at this point, so it's wise to position a bucket underneath.

I HAVE TO SAY I'M NOT NUTS ABOUT THIS JOB.

6 Unhook the lift rod from the flushing lever and lift out the siphon. Take the flap off the plate and replace it with a new one. If necessary, use a pair of scissors to cut it to the correct size.

7 Put the pieces back together again, reversing the order in which you took them apart. Don't get your nuts mixed up – never a good idea. Reassemble the flushing mechanism, reattach the flush pipe, then untie the float arm to let the cistern fill with water.

8 Cross your fingers and test the flush.

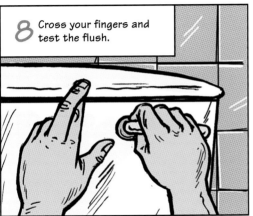

YAY! THE FLUSH IS WORKING...BUT WHAT'S THIS? IT WON'T STOP FILLING AND THE WATER LEVEL'S TOO HIGH NOW. RATS! THAT MEANS I NEED TO ADJUST THE BALL VALVE...

TO BE CONTINUED

9 In most toilets, the float arm is responsible for opening and closing the valve that lets water into the cistern. When the toilet is flushed, the cistern empties and the float arm drops down, thus opening the valve to let it refill. When the float reaches the correct level, the valve closes.

10 If, for some reason, the float is not rising high enough to shut the ball valve, water will keep on flowing continuously. If this happens to you, first of all remove the float and check that it hasn't filled up with water, making it too heavy.

NOPE, NO WATER IN MY BALL. THAT'S NOT THE REASON WHY THE CISTERN'S OVERFLOWING.

11 Try bending the float arm down slightly so that the float will rise sooner and shut off the ball valve. If you can't bend it by hand, use pliers.

CAPTAIN'S TIP
If the float is shutting off the water before the cistern has filled completely, try bending the float arm upwards.

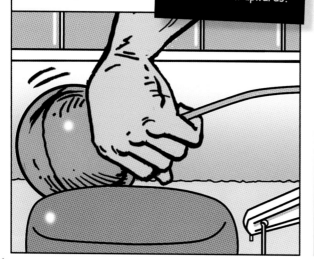

12 Just to complicate things, some modern cisterns have a plastic float arm and the valve is fitted with an adjustable screw to regulate the water entering the cistern. If this is the case in your loo, release the lock nut and turn the screw towards the valve to lower the water level and away from the valve to raise it.

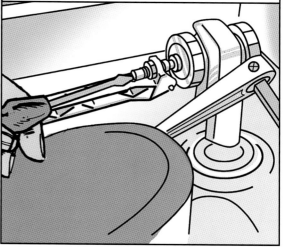

13 If the cistern still keeps refilling after you've adjusted the float arm, it probably means your ball valve needs a new washer. To fit it, you will have to turn off the water supply to the cistern, either by turning off the main stopcock or the lavatory cistern valve, and flush to empty it. Take out the pin holding the valve under the float arm and put it to one side.

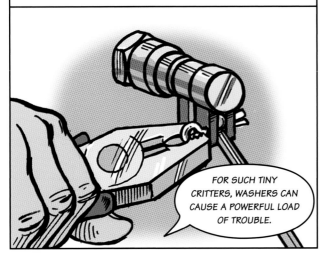

FOR SUCH TINY CRITTERS, WASHERS CAN CAUSE A POWERFUL LOAD OF TROUBLE.

14 Insert a screwdriver into the slot beneath the valve body and slide the piston out. Unscrew the end cap with pliers and pick out the old washer.

15 When you've taken all the pieces apart, it's worth giving them a bit of a scrub before you put them back together again. Use wire wool to clean the piston, then wrap some fine abrasive paper around the end of a pencil and use it to clean gently inside the valve body.

16 Fit the nice new washer, reassemble the valve and connect the float arm again. We're on the home straight now, guys.

17 Restore the water supply and adjust the float arm until the water stops at the correct level – 25 mm (1 in) below the top of the overflow outlet.

WITH HIS SUPERHERO BRAIN POWER AND EXTRAORDINARY DEXTERITY, AS WELL AS STRENGTH, RESOURCEFULNESS AND CUSTOMARY MODESTY, THE CAPTAIN TRIUMPHS AGAIN!

WATER ON TAP

A HANDYMAN'S WORK IS NEVER DONE. AROUND EVERY CORNER LURK MORE CHORES. HEY, CAP-TAIN!

1 When Kevin gets home from Caroline's, he decides to freshen up, but as he enters the bathroom he hears an ominous 'drip, drip' sound and realizes his bath tap is dripping.

2 The two most common kinds of non-mixer tap are the traditional pillar tap, with a separate handle and bell-shaped cover; and modern shrouded-head tap where the head and cover are in one piece.

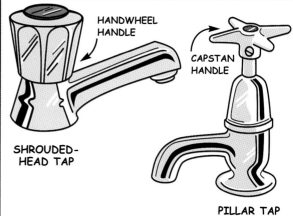

HANDWHEEL HANDLE

CAPSTAN HANDLE

SHROUDED-HEAD TAP

PILLAR TAP

CAPTAIN'S TIP
Put the plug in your sink, or line it with a hand towel, so that you don't accidentally drop any vital little pieces down the plughole.

SUPERHEROES CAN UNSCREW TAP COVERS WITH THEIR BARE HANDS, BUT YOU MAY NEED TO USE A WRENCH WITH THE TEETH WRAPPED IN MASKING TAPE TO PROTECT THE TAP FROM DAMAGE.

3 Turn off the water supply, turn the tap to the fully on position, then prise off the cover of your tap with a screwdriver and undo the retaining screw.

4 Use an adjustable spanner to unscrew the headgear from the body of the tap. The washer will be underneath, either attached to the jumper valve plate or lying inside the body of the tap. It may be attached to the jumper by a small retaining nut, which you'll have to unscrew.

5 Prise off the old washer with a knife or screwdriver and replace it with one of the same size. (They'll be able to match it if you take it to your local DIY shop.)

IF YOU DON'T HAVE A NEW WASHER, TRY TURNING THE OLD ONE OVER. IT COULD LAST A GOOD WHILE LONGER.

6 While you are replacing a washer, have a look at the valve seating. If it is worn out, or covered in scale, the watertight seal won't work and your tap will keep on dripping, even with a new washer. There are two ways to deal with this problem.

ALTERNATIVES

Option one is to hire a reseating tool from your handiest DIY shop and use it to grind the seat flat. You just screw the tool into the body of the tap, adjust the cutter, then turn the handle to smooth the metal. Be nice and firm.

Or you can cover the old seating with a new plastic liner that is sold with its own matching jumper and washer. It slips inside the old metal seat and is forced into place when the tap is turned off.

I ALWAYS MAKE SURE MY JUMPER MATCHES.

7 As you put the taps back together again, it's a good idea to grease the threads with petroleum jelly. Turn the tap off before you reinstate the water supply.

WE'VE FIXED KEVIN'S BATH TAP NOW, BUT I'M A BIT WORRIED ABOUT HIS GLANDS... SO THERE ARE MORE NAIL-BITING TAP DRAMAS ON THE NEXT PAGES!

CONTINUED OVER

DOES THAT BOY HAVE ANY TAPS THAT WORK PROPERLY?

8 Just as he's finished fixing the bath tap, the Captain notices that one of the taps in Kevin's basin is leaking from the spindle.

9 For this job, you need the tap turned off, but <u>not</u> the water. Undo the small screw that holds the capstan handle in place and remove the cover to reveal the gland nut at the top of the spindle. You could try simply tightening the gland nut to fix the problem, but – never one to do anything by halves – the Captain decides to replace the packing that keeps the nut watertight.

BE CAREFUL WITH THE TINY SCREW THAT HOLDS THE CAPSTAN HANDLE IN PLACE. IT'S REMARKABLY EASY TO LOSE.

10 Packing can be string, hemp, impregnated twine – or a rubber O-ring (see opposite). Remove the gland nut, rake out the old packing and replace it with the new. The Captain chooses a twine made from the plumber's favourite PTFE tape. Wind the new packing around your spindle and push it into the gland using the tip of a screwdriver.

THAT'S MY GLAND PACKED, SO NOW I CAN SCREW MY HEAD BACK ON.

TUT, TUT. NO TIME FOR TEA! THE KITCHEN TAP IS LEAKING AS WELL!

11 The Captain unscrews the retaining screw that holds the kitchen mixer spout in place. If your mixer tap doesn't have a screw like this, turn it to line up with the tap body, then give it a good hard yank.

12 All mixer taps have rubber O-rings instead of packing. Note their positions then take them to your DIY shop to get exact replacements.

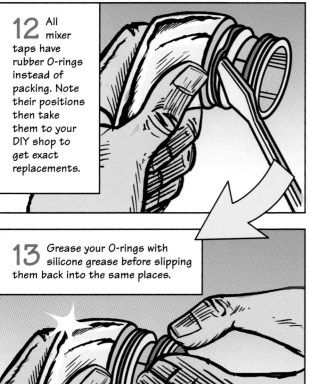

13 Grease your O-rings with silicone grease before slipping them back into the same places.

14 Refit the spout, turn on the tap and fill your kettle. Put a teabag in boiling water...

THE CAPTAIN MAY BE GOOD AT FIXING TAPS, BUT I NOTICE HE NEVER DEIGNS TO MAKE THE TEA HIMSELF.

REJUVENATING YOUR BATH

EUWW, GROSS!

Kevin fancies a nice long soak to ease the cares of the day, but once he's started to notice the shortcomings around his house, it seems that ever more appear. Staring him in the face is a stained old bath that doesn't look clean enough to get into. And the sealant around the edge looks pretty dingy, too. Kevin is not a happy bunny.

BEFORE YOU GO TO ALL THE TROUBLE OF RAKING OUT YOUR GROUT AND RESEALING THE BATH, WHY DON'T YOU TRY A PROPRIETARY GROUT CLEANER? IT WILL REMOVE MINOR STAINS AND BLACK MOULD. YOU'VE PROBABLY GOT BLACK MOULD...

GROUTO

WHAT IF MY SEALANT IS JUST TOO GROTTY?

YOU CAN BUY A PROPRIETARY SEALANT REMOVER; JUST PAINT IT ON, LEAVE FOR 15 MINUTES, THEN SCRAPE OFF THE OLD SEALANT WITH A KNIFE. CLEAN AND DEGREASE THE AREA WITH WHITE SPIRIT, THEN APPLY NEW FLEXIBLE SEALANT IN A CONTINUOUS STRIP.

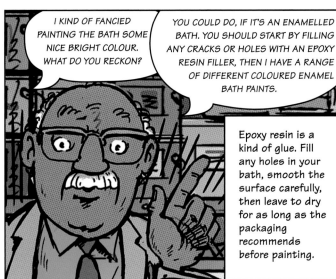

Epoxy resin is a kind of glue. Fill any holes in your bath, smooth the surface carefully, then leave to dry for as long as the packaging recommends before painting.

SHOWER POWER
UNCLOGGING THE HEAD

I GIVE UP! THIS NEW PLUG WON'T FIT. CAPTAIN COMPETENT, I NEED YOU AGAIN

IT WOULD NEVER OCCUR TO KEVIN TO TRY USING A TOOL, LIKE THESE PLIERS. HE EXPECTS EVERYTHING TO SNAP INTO PLACE LIKE PRESS STUDS.

The Captain examines all the goods that Kevin has brought home from the DIY shop and scratches his head in bewilderment. Few of them seem particularly useful.

WHAT ON EARTH DID HE GET ENAMEL BATH PAINT FOR? HIS BATH'S MADE OF PLASTIC! THE ONLY THING THAT'S USEFUL IN HERE IS THE GROUT CLEANER. BUT HANG ON A MINUTE... I KNOW WHAT WE CAN USE THAT LIMESCALE REMOVER FOR.

1 Kevin's shower head is clogged up with limescale deposits, which can be a real problem in hard-water areas, making the spray go all over the place.

THIS SHOWER'S USEFUL FOR CLEANING THE CEILING, BUT NOT SO GREAT FOR RINSING SHAMPOO FROM YOUR HAIR.

2 Remove the shower head from the hose, or just slip out the perforated plate from the head. Soak it in a proprietary limescale remover or, if you don't have any, try vinegar.

3 Use a toothpick or a needle to poke limescale build-up out of all the little holes before you reattach your shower head. Rinse the shower head through thoroughly before you use it again.

PAH! I HATE THE FIDDLY LITTLE JOBS. I FEEL LIKE A GRIZZLY BEAR TRYING TO DO CROSS-STITCH.

4 If your shower head is still clogged, it's time to buy a new one from the DIY store. Take the old one to make sure you get a match.

KEVIN COULD GET A POWER SHOWER INSTALLED HERE, BUT HE'D BETTER NOT EVEN THINK ABOUT DOING IT HIMSELF. REMEMBER WHAT WE SAID ABOUT WATER AND ELECTRICITY? AND WHO WAS IT WHO FUSED HIS HOUSE WHEN HE TRIED TO CHANGE A KETTLE PLUG? NUFF SAID.

SEE PAGE 216 FOR ADVICE ON FINDING A GOOD PLUMBER.

TAKE A SEAT

1 Kevin is cleaning his bath for the first time ever, and is amazed at how brightly it sparkles. Avoid abrasive bath cleaners, that might scratch the surface, and always use ecologically friendly products if you're worried about possible pollution.

CAPTAIN'S KIT
* replacement toilet seat
* adjustable/cranked
* spanner
* screwdriver

2 Kneeling on the toilet seat is one of the most reliable ways of breaking it.

3 Toilet seats and lids are usually attached to hinged rods at the back, which slot into hinge covers at the sides. Each is held in place by a fixing bolt in the back of the pan, secured by a wing nut underneath. You may need a spanner to release the nut, but then you'll find the rest comes apart quite simply.

I'D BETTER MAKE SURE I GET MY NUTS IN THE RIGHT PLACE. MAYBE I'LL PUT THE TOOLBELT ON, JUST FOR A MOMENT.

4 The Captain only takes a few seconds to install the toilet seat, by inserting the bolts, then screwing them to the pan. He makes sure he includes the washers supplied to protect the pan from the securing bolts and wing nuts.

NO NEED FOR A SPANNER. JUST SCREW THE WING NUTS AS TIGHT AS YOU CAN BY HAND.

5 Always test the seat to make sure it's not wobbling and that it rests centrally over the pan.

YOU COULD CALL ME THE POWER BEHIND THE THRONE!

IS THAT IT? HAVE I FINISHED ALL THE WORK THAT NEEDS TO BE DONE IN HERE?

6 Eagle-eyed readers will spot the obvious flaw that still needs to be fixed. To see what becomes of Kevin's eccentrically wonky tiling, skip to pages 160–5.

CHAPTER 3 PRESENTS...

CAPTAIN COMPETENT'S

WORKING WITH WOOD

A house without wood is like fish without chips, eggs without bacon, or Kevin without the Captain — in other words, a bit useless! Here we're going to explain how you can enhance the wood in your home and add some attractive new wooden features, such as stunning shelves, fantastic floorboards and unscruffy skirting. If you've read the earlier advice on Happy Hammering and Careful Cutting, you'll soon have all your wood looking (and sounding) wonderful...

SQUEAKY BOARDS
FIX THEM DOWN

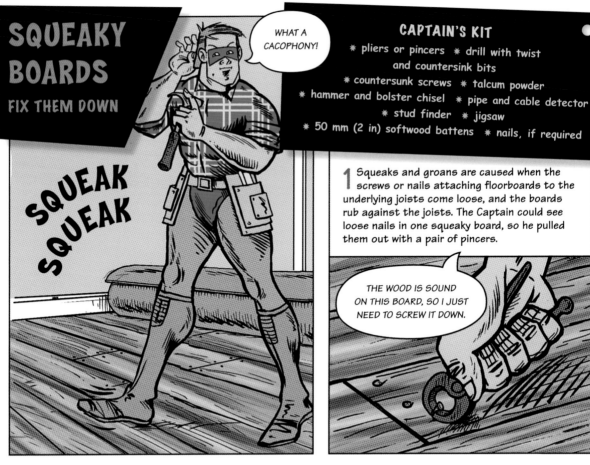

SQUEAK SQUEAK

WHAT A CACOPHONY!

CAPTAIN'S KIT
* pliers or pincers * drill with twist and countersink bits
* countersunk screws * talcum powder
* hammer and bolster chisel * pipe and cable detector
* stud finder * jigsaw
* 50 mm (2 in) softwood battens * nails, if required

1 Squeaks and groans are caused when the screws or nails attaching floorboards to the underlying joists come loose, and the boards rub against the joists. The Captain could see loose nails in one squeaky board, so he pulled them out with a pair of pincers.

THE WOOD IS SOUND ON THIS BOARD, SO I JUST NEED TO SCREW IT DOWN.

2 No need to check for pipes and cables if you're drilling into the previous holes. Use a countersink drill bit afterwards, so the screw heads are flush with the floor surface.

CAPTAIN'S TIP
Sprinkle a little talcum powder between your floorboards. Not only does it help to stop them squeaking, but also it will make them smell lovely!

3 Another board is so damaged at the edges that it would be impossible to insert new nails, so the Captain decides to replace it. There is a convenient joint nearby where he can insert the flat edge of a bolster chisel and use it to lever up the board. (If you have tongue-and-groove floorboards that slot into each other, the job will be more complicated, as you'll have to cut through the tongues – see page 125 to find out how tongue-and-groove boards are fitted together.)

WITH ALL THE WORK THAT NEEDS TO BE DONE IN KEVIN'S HOUSE, I'LL NEVER GET 'BOARD'. HA, HA!

4 If there is no joint nearby, or if the board disappears under skirting, for example, you will have to saw through the board to get your chisel underneath. First of all, use a pipe and cable detector to figure out where the pipe runs are and mark them in pencil on the boards. Now use a stud finder to locate the nearest joist. Drill through the board beside the joist to make a starter hole, then cut across it with a jigsaw or padsaw.

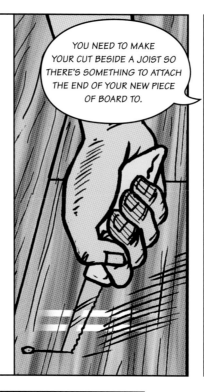

YOU NEED TO MAKE YOUR CUT BESIDE A JOIST SO THERE'S SOMETHING TO ATTACH THE END OF YOUR NEW PIECE OF BOARD TO.

5 Slip the edge of the chisel under the board and gently start to loosen the nails, taking care not to damage any surrounding boards. As you work along the length, slip a wooden wedge, or the handle of the hammer, underneath to help release the nails farther along.

DON'T TRY TO FORCE IT FASTER THAN IT WANTS TO COME.

6 When the damaged board has been lifted out, remove any remaining nails and brush out debris, then cut the new board to the correct length. You'll have to nail a batten to the side of the joist so you can secure the end of the new board to it. Make sure it fits tightly underneath the adjoining boards.

IF YOUR REPLACEMENT BOARD IS TOO WIDE FOR THE GAP, JUST CUT IT DOWN TO FIT.

7 Nail down floorboards, using nails that are long enough to go through their thickness and at least 25 mm (1 in) into the batten below. Alternatively, the Captain is using countersunk screws because there are pipes underneath this board that he might need to get access to in future.

WE'RE NOT THROUGH WITH FLOORBOARDS YET. SEE PAGES 110-13 FOR SOME SENSATIONAL FINISHES YOU CAN APPLY TO YOUR WOOD.

CREAKY STAIRS
SHUT THEM UP!

SQUEAK

SOUNDS LIKE THE FROGS' CHORUS ON THESE STAIRS.

CAPTAIN'S KIT
* drill with twist and countersink bits
* long screws * screwdriver
* wood filler and filling knife
* abrasive paper
* sanding block * wood glue
* wedges of wood
* chisel * brackets, if required

1 It's not just Kevin's hall that is noisy – his stairs make loud creaking noises at different points. Stairs are made of treads (the bits you put your foot on) and risers (the vertical bits that lead up to the next step). They creak when the joints between treads and risers have come loose. Walk up and down a few times, trying to hear whether your creaks come from the front or back of a step, or all over.

2 The first question to decide when fixing creaking stairs is whether you can get access to work from underneath the staircase. This would give a more discreet finish and, if your stairs are carpeted, it will save the effort of lifting the carpet. If it's plastered under the stairs, or otherwise inaccessible, you'll have to work from above.

3 If it seems to be the front of a step that's causing the problem, you might be able to solve it by inserting screws through the front of the tread into the riser below. Drill clearance holes down through the tread to take the shank of the screw, then countersink your screw so that the threaded bit goes into the riser below and the head is flush with the surface of the tread. You must take care to position the screws so they go into the centre of the riser's top edge.

4 Fill the screw holes with wood filler to disguise the screw heads, then sand them smooth. If they are not going to be covered with carpet, touch them up with an appropriate finish so they blend in with the wood round about.

5 If it seems to be the back of your step that is creaking, there must be a gap where the tread reaches its next upward riser. To fill it, cut some thin triangular wedges of wood, coat them in wood glue, then hammer them in between the tread and riser. Use a chisel to cut off the excess pieces of wedge.

TWO OR THREE WEDGES WILL BE ENOUGH UNLESS YOUR STEP IS VERY WIDE

6 If you can see gaps between your wedges, glue on some strips of wooden moulding to fill them. Alternatively, you could fit an angle bracket at each side of the step to hold it in place.

CAPTAIN'S TIP

You'll find a huge selection of wooden mouldings on sale in your local DIY store, and there are many different uses for them. They are used to trim between floor and skirting board, and to keep the glass in place in glazed doors and windows — as well as fixing stairs.

ALTERNATIVELY

1 If you can get under your stairs, you can screw in some supports to join the offending tread and riser together. You'll need two or three triangular wooden blocks per step. Each of them should be about 75 mm (3 in) long and 38 mm (1½ in) in depth.

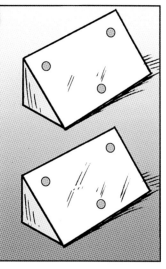

2 Hold each block in place at the junction of the tread and riser. Choose a suitably sized drill bit and drill pilot holes: two upwards into the tread above, and one horizontally into the riser.

MY FATHER WAS A SUPERHERO AS WELL. YOU COULD CALL ME A CHIP OFF THE OLD BLOCK!

3 Spread wood glue over the two surfaces of the block that meet the tread and riser, then insert screws that are long enough to penetrate into the tread and riser, but won't break through the wood on the other side.

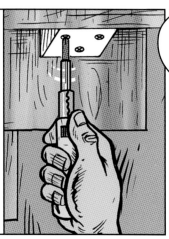

WATCH YOU DON'T GET GLUE IN YOUR HAIR WHILE WORKING UNDER THE STAIRS. JUST TRYING TO WARN YOU ABOUT EVERY POSSIBLE EVENTUALITY.

4 Squeeze glue into any other cracks that you can see — and don't use the stairs again until the glue has dried.

KEEP THE WINDOWS OPEN FOR VENTILATION, BUT SEAL OFF THE DOORS INTO THE REST OF THE HOUSE WITH MASKING TAPE. OH, AND DRAPE THE CABLE OVER YOUR SHOULDER WHILE YOU'RE WORKING SO YOU DON'T ACCIDENTALLY GO OVER IT...

I THINK THAT'S ME ALL READY TO START... BUT MAYBE I'D BETTER PUT MY TOOLBELT ON, JUST TO BE ON THE SAFE SIDE.

The Old Man was still talking when Kevin rushed out, eager to get home and make a start.

1 Before you begin sanding, make sure there aren't any nails protruding from the floor or you'll rip your abrasive paper. If you find some, tap them down below the surface using a hammer and nail punch. Pull out any remaining carpet tacks with a tack lifter. Fix any loose boards, just as we did on pages 102–3, and fill any gaps between boards with narrow strips of wood glued into place, or use a cartridge-type wood filler. Get your surface as level as you can.

TUT, TUT. KEVIN HASN'T DONE HIS PREPARATION AT ALL. GOOD PREPARATION AND A GOOD FINISH ARE THE KEYS TO A PROFESSIONAL-LOOKING DIY TASK. OH, AND GOOD WORK IN BETWEEN.

I STRONGLY ADVISE ONE LAST TRIP TO THE TOILET BEFORE YOU SEAL YOURSELF IN THE ROOM. AND MAKE SURE YOU'VE GOT EVERYTHING YOU NEED INSIDE.

2 Sweep the floor thoroughly, then seal your doors with masking tape to prevent dust escaping all over the house. Make sure your windows are open to give plenty of ventilation.

3 Fit a sheet of coarse abrasive paper into the sander, put on your safety gear, and you're ready to roll.

LET'S GET THIS SHOW ON THE ROAD.

4 If your boards are fairly level, you can skip steps 4 and 5, and go straight to step 6. If your boards are uneven, with raised edges, begin in one corner of the room and sand the boards in diagonal lines. Tilt the drum sander backwards, turn on the power, then gently lower it to the floor.

DON'T LET THE SANDER RUN AWAY FROM YOU. KEEP A FIRM HOLD, BECAUSE IT WILL PROPEL ITSELF FORWARDS. TILT IT BACKWARDS EVERY TIME YOU WANT TO TURN AROUND, OR SWITCH IT OFF.

5 When you reach a wall, tilt the drum, turn it around, and work back parallel to and slightly overlapping your last run. When you've sanded one diagonal, do the same on the opposite diagonal.

DON'T WORRY ABOUT CORNERS AND EDGES FOR NOW. WE'LL TACKLE THEM LATER.

6 Sweep up the dust. Unplug the sander and fit a medium-grade abrasive sheet. Now sand again in overlapping parallel runs along the length of the boards.

SANDING ACROSS THE GRAIN OF THE WOOD CAN LEAVE SCORES THAT ARE HARD TO REMOVE.

7 Same routine: sweep up, unplug the sander, then change to a fine-grade paper. Work along the grain of the floorboards again.

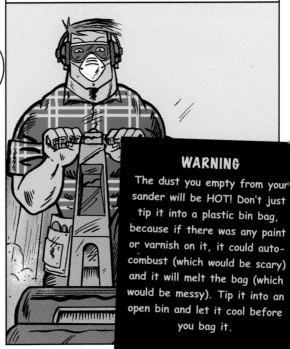

WARNING

The dust you empty from your sander will be HOT! Don't just tip it into a plastic bin bag, because if there was any paint or varnish on it, it could auto-combust (which would be scary) and it will melt the bag (which would be messy). Tip it into an open bin and let it cool before you bag it.

8 Now it's time to sand the edges. Do this with an edging sander and move down through the grades of paper, from coarse to medium to fine. Keep the sander moving, or you could gouge a hole in the floor! If you have any awkward inaccessible areas, you could use a smaller hand sander or abrasive paper wrapped around a sanding block.

THIS IS WHERE THE KNEE PROTECTORS COME IN HANDY.

9 Nearly there! Dust all the shelves, ledges above doors and windows, and the tops of skirting, then vacuum thoroughly. Wipe down your boards with a damp mop and let them dry.

WHO ARE YOU CALLING A SUCKER?

10 Now wipe the floor with white spirit, using a lint-free cloth.

11 Hey presto! One smooth wooden floor! But the job's not done yet, because the wood needs to be sealed to protect it. See over the page for advice on the wide range of finishes you can choose from...

FLOORBOARD FINISHES
KEVIN'S DILEMMA

DO I WANT MY WOOD TO LOOK SUPER-WOODY, MEDIUM WOODY OR LESS WOODY?

Kevin can't make up his mind what kind of finish he wants. The sitting room floorboards are slightly uneven in colour and they also need to be sealed to protect them from spills and bumps. Kevin buys sample sizes of several different finishes and decides to try them out on a spare board. (If you're doing this, note that new wood and old wood will take stains differently.)

Bleaching will lighten dark woods – or dark stained patches in one area. Proprietary wood bleaches are sometimes sold as two-step products – one to start the fading process and another to stop it. If they're not two-step, you'll need to neutralize the bleach with vinegar to stop the lightening process. Wear protective gloves to keep it off your skin. Remember that the wood will look paler when it dries, so don't go too far. Rinse your floor with clean water afterwards and allow to dry.

THE BLEACHED LOOK IS A BIT TOO PALE TO CAMOUFLAGE SPILT COFFEE.

I LIKE THIS, BUT SOMEHOW I'M NOT SURE THAT CAROLINE WOULD.

You can paint your floorboards with a solid colour of your choice, but bear in mind that this will mask the natural grain of the wood. Use a long-handled roller to apply floor paints, but don't overload it or paint will seep into the cracks between the boards. Two or three thin coats are best. You can even paint or stencil on patterns if you want to be totally wacky! (Bad idea, Kevin.)

For a coloured paint effect that still lets the features of the wood show through, why not try colour-washing? There are lots of ready-made colour washes available on the market, but you can make your own by diluting emulsion paint with water until it is a thin, milky consistency. The more water you add, the more transparent the finish will be. Apply with a long-handled roller, as for floor paints; you'll find it will dry more quickly than undiluted paint, so don't dilly-dally.

I ALWAYS WANTED TO PAINT THE TOWN RED, AND THIS COULD BE THE START.

SEE PAGES 136–149 for lots more tricks and tips on painting!

I DON'T THINK I'M GOING TO GIVE THIS ONE THE GREEN LIGHT.

Wood stains help to even out colour across a patchy floor while still showing off the features of the wood. There are dozens of shades available, from subtle honey-coloured tints through to deep cherry woods and rich walnuts. Apply the stain with a sponge or soft cloth, working in the direction of the grain. Don't overlap any areas or they will come out darker than the rest. Let the first coat dry, then apply another if you want to deepen the effect. And do stay away from garish shades.

Whether you've chosen bleach, paint, colour-wash or a stain, you'll need to apply varnish as a protective top coat. Choose from clear or tinted varnish, with gloss, matt or satin finishes. Matt shows the patterns of the wood graining best; gloss is too reflective. You can also choose between water-based varnishes that are milky in appearance, but dry to a clear finish, and oil-based polyurethane ones that dry with a slightly yellowish tinge, but are much harder-wearing. See over the page for varnishing instructions – and to find out what Kevin chose. (Why does my heart sink at the thought?)

EENY-MEENY MINY-MO, CATCH A SUPERHERO AND DON'T LET HIM GO...

A VARNISHING ACT...

WITHOUT STICKY FINGERS

THIS SHOULD MAKE HER HAPPY. BUT IT ALL LOOKS LIKE HARD WORK, SO PERHAPS I'LL LET CAPTAIN COMPETENT DO IT!

CAPTAIN'S KIT
* wood stain
* sponge
* varnish paintbrush
* protective mask and gloves
* white spirit
* fine-grade abrasive paper
* lint-free cloth
* wire wool

1 Racked with indecision about his floor finish, Kevin comes across the magazine Caroline had shown him and locates the picture she'd pointed out. The floor in it is finished with a classy beech stain and coated with clear matt varnish. Ever-anxious to please his fabulous girlfriend, Kevin decides to do the same. Huge sigh of relief all round.

START IN THE CORNER OF THE ROOM FARTHEST FROM THE DOOR AND WORK BACKWARDS. DON'T MAKE THE MISTAKE THAT KEVIN ONCE MADE WHEN STAINING HIS MOTHER'S FLOOR...

HE WAS STUCK THERE ALL DAY WAITING FOR THE STAIN TO DRY.

DON'T LET ANYONE USE A NAKED FLAME NEARBY WHEN YOU'RE WORKING WITH FLAMMABLE VARNISH. THIS ISN'T THE PLACE FOR PYROTECHNICS.

3 Once the stain has dried (check the recommended drying time on the packaging), you will be ready to varnish. Use a brand new, good-quality 75 or 100 mm (3 or 4 in) paintbrush. For solvent-based varnish, it can help to spread the first coat more easily if you thin it with one part white spirit to ten parts of varnish (you can thin acrylic varnish with water).

2 First, the Captain makes sure the room is well ventilated because the fumes from some wood finishes can be unpleasant to inhale. He puts on his protective mask. Gloves are a good idea too, if only to stop you getting indelible stains all over your paws. Apply the stain evenly with a sponge.

4 Apply the first coat of varnish, brushing in the direction of the grain. After it has dried, rub away any dust specks or shed bristles with a piece of abrasive paper and wipe these areas clean using a lint-free cloth dipped in white spirit.

5 Apply a second coat of unthinned varnish. If you're lazy, you can stop here, but a true perfectionist like Captain Competent will wait for the second coat to dry before rubbing gently over the floor surface with a wire wool pad.

6 At last, he applies the final coat and stands back to admire his own work.

When Caroline comes around later, she can't believe her eyes.

NEWS FLASH...
What should Kevin do? How can he persuade her that he's still the same clumsy old Kev? Or should he confess about the toolbelt and his superhero alter ego?

NO-SWEAT FLOORBOARDS

LAYING WOODSTRIP FLOORING

GOOD GRIEF! WHAT'S THAT DOING THERE?

1 Glowing with excitement about his spectacular sitting room floor, Kevin decides to try the same effect in the dining room. But when he lifts the carpet, he gets a shock – it's concrete underneath!

... I REALLY WANTED ANOTHER WOODEN FLOOR AND NOW I DON'T KNOW WHAT TO DO.

2 What he needs is laminate woodstrip flooring. The locking kind just slots together and doesn't need to be nailed or glued in place. You can also get tongue-and-groove woodstrip, but it has to be glued and it's virtually impossible to lift if you ever need to replace a board.

HERE ARE ALL THE BITS AND PIECES YOU'LL NEED FOR YOUR DINING ROOM FLOOR. PLUS, AHEM, FULL INSTRUCTIONS. I STRONGLY RECOMMEND THAT YOU READ THEM.

3 First of all you need an underlay. The Old Man gives Kevin one that is combined with a damp-proof membrane, which is essential on concrete floors to stop damp seeping through and warping your boards. You'll need to calculate the area of the room to see how much woodstrip you need. And the woodstrip fitting kit contains everything else – expansion spacers, a tapping block and pulling bar (we'll explain about them later).

4 Leave your woodstrip to acclimatize in the room where it will be used for at least 48 hours. Meanwhile, check your floor with a spirit level to make sure there are no serious dips, bumps or slopes, which would cause the woodstrip to bend. If you need to get a concrete floor levelled, call in a builder to smooth on a floor-levelling compound.

I DON'T BELIEVE IT! AT LAST I'VE FOUND SOMETHING IN KEVIN'S HOUSE THAT ISN'T CROOKED!

5 Lay the sheets of underlay flat across the surface of the floor and tape the pieces together with some strong adhesive tape. Use scissors to cut the underlay to fit.

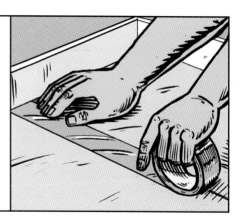

6 Choose the longest, straightest wall in the room to start with and lay your first plank. Insert spacers to ensure that there is a gap of 6 mm (¼ in) between the plank and the wall. Wood expands naturally in different temperatures and at different humidity levels, so it needs this space to expand into.

I'VE PUT MY KNEE PROTECTORS ON. IT WOULD BE HUMILIATING FOR A DIY SUPERHERO TO GET HOUSEMAID'S KNEE.

7 Different types of woodstrip can slot together in different ways, but the type Kevin has chosen locks very simply. Slip the short tongue at the end of your second plank over the long tongue of the first board, tilting it at an angle of about 30°, then lower it to lock it into place.

ANY CHILD WHO CAN LAY OUT TRACK FOR THEIR TOY TRAINS COULD DO THIS PART OF THE JOB.

8 When you reach the end of the first row, you'll almost certainly have to cut a plank to fit. Here's how: turn the plank around so its short tongue is 6 mm (¼ in) from the end wall (insert a spacer) and it is lying next to the previous plank. Use a try square and pencil to mark a cutting line across the end plank. Put on a mask and goggles to cut it to size with a jigsaw. It will be laid so that the cut end is against the wall, where it will be hidden from view.

115

9 To lay the last piece in a row, you need to use your nifty pulling bar. It has a short lip turned over at one end and a longer lip at the other. Slip the short lip over the cut end of your last plank (the end that will be nearest the wall), then tap with a hammer on the longer lip to slot the last plank into the previous one. You'll repeat this at the end of each row; otherwise it could drive you crazy trying to slot that fiddly end bit neatly into place.

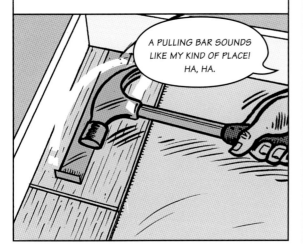

A PULLING BAR SOUNDS LIKE MY KIND OF PLACE! HA, HA.

10 The second row of woodstrip will lock into the first if you tilt the long edge at an angle to the long edge of the first row, then lower the plank into place. It is best if you stagger the joints between planks from row to row, so start row 2 with the offcut from row 1. Hold a tapping block against the edges and tap it with a hammer to make snug joints without damaging the boards.

DON'T EVER HAMMER WOODSTRIP DIRECTLY, OR YOU'LL DAMAGE THE EDGES AND WILL HAVE TO REPLACE THE BOARD.

11 When you reach the wall opposite the one where you started, you will have to cut your planks to the correct width. Place each on top of its neighbour in the previous row. Butt the long edge of another plank up to the wall and use a pencil to mark the cutting line on the middle plank, remembering to allow for the expansion gap. Cut your planks with a jigsaw and lay them so that the cut edge is against the wall. Use your good old pulling bar to slot them securely into place.

AS YOU GO ALONG, FROM TIME TO TIME, CHECK EVERYTHING IS STRAIGHT AND LEVEL, USING YOUR TRY SQUARE AND SPIRIT LEVEL.

12 Where the architrave around a door frame protrudes into the room, it is neater to trim it and slide the flooring underneath than to try and cut your woodstrip to the exact shape. Lay an offcut of woodstrip butting up to the architrave and rest a panel saw flat on top of it. Cut into the architrave. Use a chisel to remove the waste piece of wood. Your woodstrip should slide in easily, but remember to allow for its 6 mm (¼ in) expansion gap along the skirting board.

MAKE SURE YOUR SAW IS SHARP, AND USE NICE EVEN STROKES. DON'T HACK AT IT.

13 Woodstrip flooring should finish underneath the door when it is in the closed position. Cut a threshold bar to the correct length and stick it down. Some should be glued, while others need to be nailed or fixed with wood screws – read the instructions.

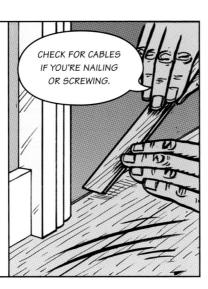

CHECK FOR CABLES IF YOU'RE NAILING OR SCREWING.

14 If you reach an obstruction, such as a radiator pipe, you'll need to measure carefully and cut out a slot to fit around it. Lay your plank in the correct position alongside the pipe, position a spacer against the wall, and measure from the front of the spacer to the front of the pipe. Do this on both sides and mark the shape on your plank. Drill a hole that matches the size of the pipe, then saw along the sides of the slot. Slide your woodstrip into place around the pipe.

FOR A SUPER-NEAT FINISH, BUY A RADIATOR PIPE COVER IN A WOOD THAT MATCHES YOUR FLOORING AND GLUE IT DOWN.

15 To finish off, cover the gaps around the edges with laminate flooring trim in a wood-effect to match your flooring. Measure and cut it to length first of all. If you've removed your skirting boards, you won't need trim – just replace them (*see page 120*).

16 Glue the back of your trim with an acrylic polymer adhesive and stick it to the skirting board, not to the flooring. Press it into place and use piles of books or other heavy objects to hold it in place until it dries. (Check the manufacturer's recommended glue drying times.)

KEEP YOUR GLUEING NEAT AND WIPE OFF ANY EXCESS IMMEDIATELY.

17 It's a good idea to put felt pads under heavy furniture so that you don't damage your woodstrip floor. Clean it by sweeping or vacuuming, and wipe it with a damp cloth if necessary.

IF YOU HAVEN'T SEEN THE FLOOR YOU WANT YET, READ ON. THERE ARE LOTS MORE TYPES TO COME.

SKIRTING TROUBLE
STICKING IT UP

UH-OH. THAT GAP BETWEEN THE SKIRTING AND THE FLOOR DOESN'T LOOK SO COOL. I GUESS THAT'S WHERE THE OLD CARPET USED TO BE.

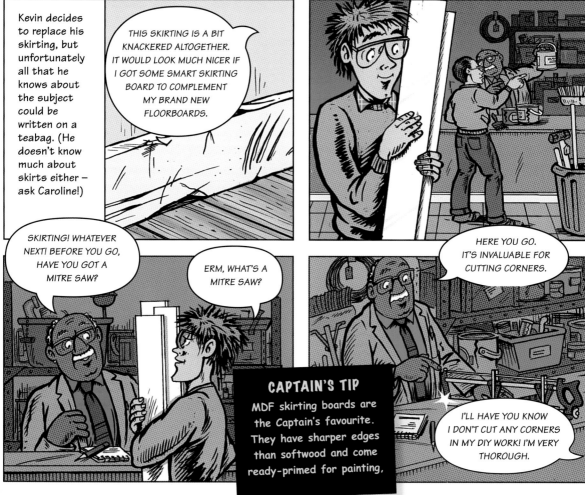

Kevin decides to replace his skirting, but unfortunately all that he knows about the subject could be written on a teabag. (He doesn't know much about skirts either – ask Caroline!)

THIS SKIRTING IS A BIT KNACKERED ALTOGETHER. IT WOULD LOOK MUCH NICER IF I GOT SOME SMART SKIRTING BOARD TO COMPLEMENT MY BRAND NEW FLOORBOARDS.

SKIRTING! WHATEVER NEXT! BEFORE YOU GO, HAVE YOU GOT A MITRE SAW?

ERM, WHAT'S A MITRE SAW?

HERE YOU GO. IT'S INVALUABLE FOR CUTTING CORNERS.

I'LL HAVE YOU KNOW I DON'T CUT ANY CORNERS IN MY DIY WORK! I'M VERY THOROUGH.

CAPTAIN'S TIP
MDF skirting boards are the Captain's favourite. They have sharper edges than softwood and come ready-primed for painting.

IT WON'T COME OFF! ALREADY THIS SKIRTING BUSINESS IS TRICKIER THAN I THOUGHT. TIME TO BRING IN CAPTAIN COMPETENT!

1 Starting in a corner, or at a joint, slip the blade of a crowbar down behind your skirting and tap it in with a hammer. Place a thin piece of wood behind the crowbar to protect your wall surface from knocks.

KEVIN HAS A FULL TOOLBOX AS WELL AS HIS MAGIC TOOLBELT, AND HE NEVER THINKS OF USING ANY OF HIS TOOLS! A CROWBAR'S WHAT YOU NEED FOR PRISING OFF SKIRTING.

2 Work along the length of the skirting, prising it away, and inserting wooden wedges if required to hold off the parts you've already freed from the wall.

I'M AN OLD HAND AT THIS. ME AND SKIRTING, WE GO WAY BACK.

3 Remove any loose nails or screws and brush away any messy debris before you put the new skirting in place.

WATCH OUT FOR LOOSE NAILS OR ONES PROTRUDING FROM THE OLD SKIRTING. YOU WON'T BE HAPPY IF YOU KNEEL ON THEM.

4 Paint the back of your new skirting board with wood preservative, then paint, stain or varnish the front, as you wish. If you have masonry walls, you can use masonry nails or screws to fix it up; oval wire nails can be driven into the studs in stud partition walls (locate them with a stud finder). If the walls are flat and true, you can use instant-grip adhesive. Fortunately, modern glues are quite strong enough to cope with this job.

5 Lay out your skirting around the room, trying to plan so that any joints will be hidden from view (behind a bookshelf or sofa, for example). Start fixing on the longest wall first. Glue the back of the skirting, press it to the wall and, if necessary, prop it in place until the glue dries.

GLUE YOUR SKIRTING TO THE WALL, NOT THE FLOOR. FLOORS NEED MORE ALLOWANCE FOR MOVEMENT, WHAT WITH WOOD SHRINKAGE AND EXPANSION, AS WELL AS HEAVY PEOPLE CLUMPING AROUND ON THEM.

6 When you reach a corner of the room, it is neatest if you mitre the boards – i.e. cut them at 45° angles so the two boards butt together neatly. This is where the mitre saw comes in. Fit the tool in a workbench or vice to hold it still. Put the skirting in the left-hand side and use the saw to cut the mitre, then put the right-hand skirting in the right-hand side and cut again. The boards go in one way for external corners and the other for internal. Look at the illustrations below right and think it through before you cut!

7 Glue the mitred joints together, as well as glueing the skirting to the wall. (Or use nails or screws, as appropriate – see step 4.)

CUT THROUGH FROM THE FRONT OF YOUR SKIRTING TOWARDS THE BACK. THAT WAY, IF THERE'S ANY SPLINTERING, IT WILL BE ON THE BACK AND WON'T SHOW.

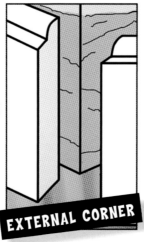

EXTERNAL CORNER

INTERNAL CORNER

There's an alternative way of cutting internal corners if you're handy with a saw – and so long as the profile (the end view) of your skirting isn't too fussy. Here's what to do: run your first piece of skirting right into the corner so that its end butts right up against the adjacent wall.

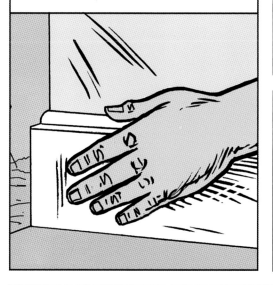

Lay the next piece of skirting face down on the floor, then hold another small piece on top of it at right angles. Trace the profile on to its back in pencil. Now you have to try to cut exactly around the profile using a coping saw.

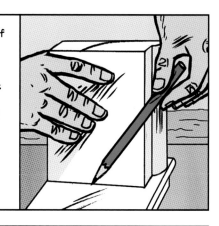

If you've made your cut accurately, your second piece will fit exactly against the first. If you haven't, try again...or go back to the mitring method, which is easier.

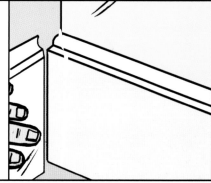

8 It's worth hammering in a couple of panel pins to supplement the glue at external corners. They can be prone to being bashed by furniture or tripped over by people like Kevin who have two left feet.

9 Now check around the room to see if there are any gaps at corners or joints. If so, fill them with a matching wood filler and sand it smooth when dry. You can fill nail or screw holes this way as well.

I DO LIKE A NICE PIECE OF SKIRT. WHOOPS, I MEAN SKIRTING...

A LITTLE LIGHT COVING

DON'T PEOPLE PUT SKIRTING BOARD AT THE TOP OF WALLS TOO?

1 As Kevin lay contemplating his fresh new skirting (yes, that's the exciting kind of life he leads), he became aware of a lack of balance in the room. The base of the walls was neatly finished, but at the top where they met the ceiling, there were paint splashes, cracks and cobwebs.

NO, KEVIN, THAT'S CALLED COVING. SAME PRINCIPLE, BUT IT'S NOT MADE OF WOOD.

2 Most types of coving are made of lightweight materials like plasterboard or expanded polystyrene. You don't want great planks of wood falling on your visitors' heads, after all.

TIME TO MOVE HOME, LITTLE SPIDERS.

3 Because of the height of the ceiling, Captain Competent decides to set up a work platform (see page 39 for more information on these). Coving is normally applied before a room is decorated. It's important to remove any loose wallpaper, flaky paint or cobwebs before you start so it has a nice clean surface to adhere to.

4 Hold up a length of coving and mark pencil lines on the ceiling and wall all around the room. If the first length (1) overlaps the second length (2), you will later cut off the excess and create a square-ended butt joint between them. If the second length doesn't meet the first, you will add a new section (3) to fit between them.

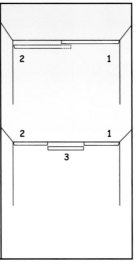

5 Scratch a few lines in the area between your ceiling and wall pencil lines, using the edge of a scraper. This will create a key for the glue.

THE KEY TO SUCCESSFUL STICKING IS A GOOD KEY.

6 Cut the mitred corners using a coving mitre box. Lay the coving in the box with the wall edge facing upwards against the side and the ceiling edge flat against the base. Use a panel saw to cut the mitres, then sand them lightly.

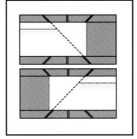

RIGHT-HAND EXTERNAL MITRE

LEFT-HAND EXTERNAL MITRE

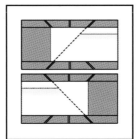

LEFT-HAND INTERNAL MITRE

RIGHT-HAND INTERNAL MITRE

7 Apply coving adhesive all along the back edges of the first piece of coving, using a spatula or trowel. There will be marks indicating which is the top edge, for sticking to the ceiling, and which is for sticking to the wall. Carefully press it into position and scrape off any adhesive that oozes out.

8 It can be a good idea to tap in a few masonry nails to hold the coving in place until the adhesive sets — but check the wall with a pipe and cable detector first. Don't want any nasty shocks, do we?

IF YOU EVER WANT TO USE YOUR SPATULA AGAIN, WIPE THE ADHESIVE OFF IT STRAIGHT AWAY, OTHERWISE, IT'S GOING TO BE HARD GLUE FOR YOU!

9 Work right around the room, sticking up your coving, then go back and fill any gaps in the corners or joints with an extra squeeze of adhesive, using your finger. You can sand it smooth when it dries.

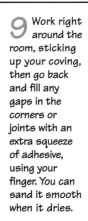

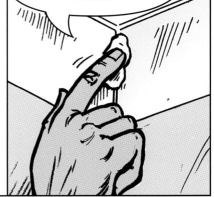

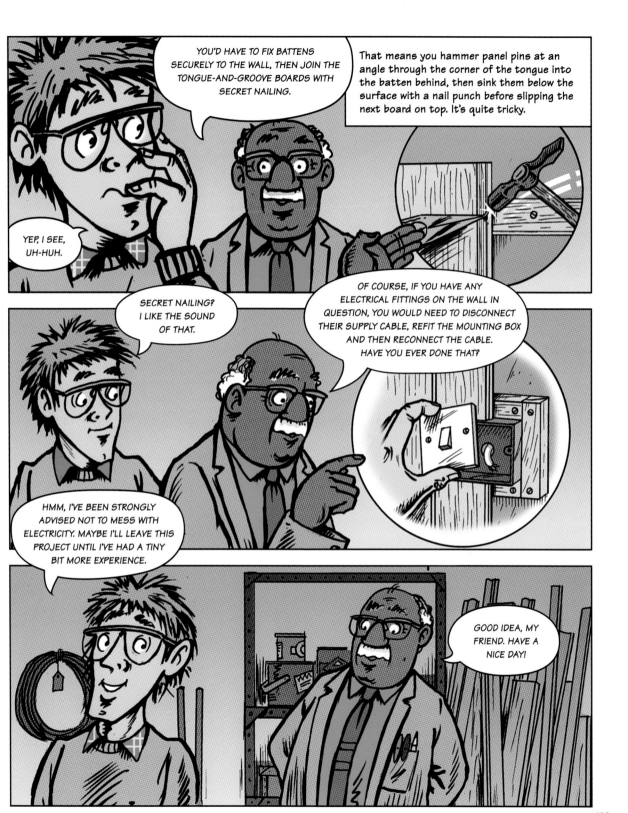

THE TRUTH ABOUT WOOD

AN INSIDER'S GUIDE

IT'S HARD TO SEE THE WOOD FOR THE TREES WHEN YOU'RE DIY-ING, BUT MY ADVICE WILL MAKE YOU MASTER CRAFTSMEN IN NO TIME. WELL, MOST OF YOU.

DO YOU LIKE YOURS SOFT OR HARD?

There are two categories of wood – softwood and hardwood – but, while the terms are generally descriptive, just to confuse you, some softwoods are harder than some hardwoods! Softwoods come from coniferous trees, like pine, fir and spruce, while hardwoods are from deciduous trees like oak, beech, mahogany and teak. In general, softwoods are cheaper and easier to work with, while hardwoods have a better surface finish so are good for furniture and decorative panelling. If the wood is not going to be on display, you could go for the cheaper option of man-made boards, such as plywood, MDF (medium-density fibreboard) or chipboard, all of them sold in sheets.

THE TROUBLE WITH PLANKS

Softwoods are sold in planks of standard length and width – but there's a catch! You can buy them 'sawn', with rough edges, or 'planed', with smooth edges. They are usually described by their sawn size. However, the planing can remove 3–5 mm (⅛– ¼ in) off each dimension, so a piece of wood sold as 100 x 50 mm (4 x 2 in) may measure only 95 x 47 mm (3¾ x 1⅞ in) in cross-section. And this could make a big difference if you're trying to get a shelf to fit across an alcove, or make doors for a fitted wardrobe. Always work with the actual wood size, not the nominal size in which it is sold.

BEWARE OF BLEMISHES

If you're buying wood, watch out for flaws. Is it bent or warped? Are there any cracks along the grain? Have any woodpeckers got their beaks into it? Does it have knots? Some people like the appearance of knots in their wood, but be aware that the wood will be weaker in that area. Also, some knots can 'bleed' resin, even through a paint top coat, unless they have been treated with knotting compound.

I HEARD THAT! WHICH ONE OF YOU CALLED ME A BLOCKHEAD???

GETTING YOUR WOOD IN THE MOOD

Allow wood to acclimatize to the humidity in your home before you work with it, or it could bend or warp as it absorbs or sheds moisture. Ideally, it should be stored horizontally, with gaps between the planks, in the room where it will be used, for several days. In practice, this could be rather inconvenient, but leave it as long as you can.

EVER GREEN

Always buy wood from sustainable sources, so that you don't bear personal responsibility for the destruction of the world's rainforests, and the ecological damage and climate change that is causing. Most DIY wood is softwood, which doesn't come from rainforests. Look for wood bearing the FSC (Forest Stewardship Council) logo – a reputable timber merchant will show you the 'sustainability' logo on the wood they sell.

WOODWORKING SAFETY

* Always wear a dust mask when cutting or drilling MDF. The dust can be harmful, so make sure you don't inhale it.

* Keep saws, planes and blades as sharp as possible (*see page 22*) and you'll find they are easier to control, as well as giving a neater finish.

* The sensitive flowers among you may want to wear goggles to stop stray specks getting in your eyes (and if you wear contact lenses, this is a good idea). Some people prefer to wear ear protectors when they're using power tools for more than a short burst. They can create a similar decibel level to that just under the speakers at a rock concert.

ON THE SHELF
DO YOU HAVE ENOUGH SUPPORT?

INTELLECTUAL CURIOSITY KILLED THE CAT, FLUFFY. THAT'LL TEACH YOU TO STAY AWAY FROM BOOK LEARNING.

WHAT ARE THEY FOR?

The first thing to decide when planning to put up new shelves is what you're going to put on them. If you design your shelves to take the little nick-nack souvenirs you brought back from your holiday, then later decide to stack an encyclopedia set on them, you're going to be in trouble...

WHAT WILL YOU NEED?

Will your new shelves take a light, medium or heavy load? Once you've made up your mind, you need to choose an appropriate shelving material, the best kind of brackets or fixings, and consult the chart opposite to decide on the best spacing for your brackets.

OF COURSE I'M STRAIGHT. WHO SAID I'M NOT?

WHICH MATERIAL?

SOLID TIMBER

Can be an expensive option, but it's strong and attractive. Treat your timber shelves with a coat of paint or varnish before you put them up.

MDF

Not as strong as timber, but it's easy to use, hence its popularity. Always wear a dust mask when cutting it to avoid inhaling nasty dust.

CHIPBOARD

Cheap and easy, but not so strong. The cheapest kind is only 16 mm (⅝ in) thick and would not support heavy loads such as books.

GLASS

Must be the toughened type for shelving and at least 6 mm (¼ in) thick. Remember that glass is heavy and will need extra support, but it will only take light loads.

When you're buying your shelving material, tell the timber merchant or glazier what it's for — even better, get them to cut it to the correct lengths for you. This is essential when buying glass shelves, which should have the edges polished so that no one has a nasty accident falling against them.

WHICH FIXINGS?

FIXED METAL OR WOOD ANGLE BRACKETS

These come in all shapes, sizes and finishes. The longer arm fixes to the wall and the shorter one to the shelf. Choose brackets with top arms that are no less than 25 mm (1 in) shorter than your shelf width.

BATTENS

Can run horizontally at the sides of an alcove for the shelf to sit on. Add one at the back to support heavy loads.

ADJUSTABLE TRACK SHELVING

Allows you to vary the height of the shelves. Cheaper systems tend to be lightweight aluminium. For heavier loads, opt for steel or wood.

BRACKET SPACING

MATERIAL	THICKNESS	LIGHT LOAD	MEDIUM LOAD	HEAVY LOAD
TIMBER	18 mm (¾ in)	800 mm (32 in)	750 mm (30 in)	700 mm (28 in)
TIMBER	25 mm (1 in)	–	915 mm (36 in)	700 mm (28 in)
CHIPBOARD	16 mm (⅝ in)	750 mm (30 in)	610 mm (24 in)	(not suitable)
CHIPBOARD	18 mm (¾ in)	–	700 mm (28 in)	510 mm (20 in)
MDF	18 mm (¾ in)	800 mm (32 in)	750 mm (30 in)	700 mm (28 in)
MDF	25 mm (1 in)	–	915 mm (36 in)	700 mm (28 in)
GLASS	6 mm (¼ in)	700 mm (28 in)	–	–

Try a quick test before you fix your shelves to the wall. Take one shelf and balance it on a couple of bricks, spaced the same distance apart that you plan to have your brackets. Place a load on the shelf of the type you intend to use it for. Check if it's sagging in the middle with a spirit level. If it is, that's what it would do on the wall – or worse!

RESCUING CAROLINE'S PIGS...
BY SHELVING HER ALCOVE

WHY DON'T I FIT SOME SHELVES IN THAT ALCOVE BESIDE YOUR FIREPLACE? YOU COULD KEEP YOUR COLLECTION OF PIGS THERE.

I'VE ALWAYS WANTED SOMEWHERE TO DISPLAY MY PIGS, BUT ARE YOU SURE YOU KNOW ABOUT SHELVING? THE ONES IN YOUR HOUSE ARE A BIT PRECARIOUS...

CAPTAIN'S KIT
* shelves * battens
* tape measure
* spirit level * drill and bits
* bradawl * screws and wallplugs
* sliding bevel * jigsaw

PROMISE ME YOU'LL TAKE PRECAUTIONS.

DON'T I ALWAYS?

1 The alcove is only 610 mm (24 in) wide, and the pigs are not very heavy, so the shelves can just rest on some battens at the sides. Timber that is 18 mm (¾ in) thick will be fine for the shelves, while the battens need to be 38 x 19 mm (1½ x ¾ in) in cross-section.

I HAVE TO MEET MY SISTER FOR A COFFEE BUT I'LL BE BACK IN A COUPLE OF HOURS. SEE YOU LATER, DARLING!

2 As soon as she's gone, Kevin puts on his toolbelt. The Captain cuts battens to fit on each side of the alcove and drills two countersunk clearance holes in each.

I'M TAKING THE MEASUREMENTS FOR EACH BATTEN INDIVIDUALLY. WALLS CAN DO VERY STRANGE THINGS...

CAPTAIN'S TIP
If you're intending to fix the shelf to the battens with screws, drill your screw clearance holes in the battens before you fix them to the wall.

3 Hold the first batten in place, using a spirit level to get it horizontal. Then, using a bradawl, mark the fixing hole positions on the wall through the holes in the batten. Alcoves are usually in chimney breast walls, which are solid, so you'll need to use 50 mm (2 in) screws and wallplugs. Drill the two holes, insert the plugs, then screw on the first batten.

SAFETY FLASH
Use your pipe and cable detector before drilling into the wall!

4 Draw pencil guidelines around the alcove and mark a fixing position for the second batten, using your spirit level to check that it is at exactly the same level as the first batten.

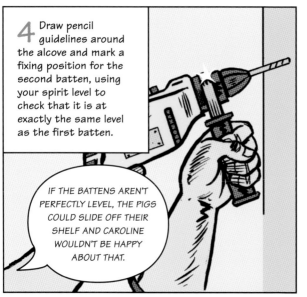

IF THE BATTENS AREN'T PERFECTLY LEVEL, THE PIGS COULD SLIDE OFF THEIR SHELF AND CAROLINE WOULDN'T BE HAPPY ABOUT THAT.

5 Now you will need to measure the angles at the corners of your alcove to make your shelves a perfect fit, and the tool to do this with is a sliding bevel. Rest the handle against the back wall of the alcove. Open the blade along the side wall to copy the angle. Cut one end of your shelf at this angle. Now measure the width at the front and back of the alcove. Mark these measurements on the shelf and join the marks. Cut the other end of your shelf and slide it into place to test the fit. If it's slightly tight, plane or sand one edge until it fits comfortably.

6 Apply the paint or varnish of your choice to the shelves. Finally, drive two countersunk screws up through the batten and into the shelf, making sure they don't break through the surface.

IF YOUR SCREWS ARE DIFFICULT TO INSERT, TRY ENLARGING THE CLEARANCE HOLES.

NEWS FLASH
If you don't have a sliding bevel, use two pieces of card instead.

KEVIN, THEY'RE BEAUTIFUL! THANK YOU SO MUCH.

THERE'S SOMETHING FISHY GOING ON AROUND HERE. I WONDER IF HE GOT SOMEONE TO HELP HIM WHILE I WAS OUT? I'M GOING TO FIND OUT!

BOOKWORMS' PARADISE
STACKING SHELVES FOR A LIBRARY

I THINK I'LL ASK KEVIN TO PUT UP SOME SHELVES IN MY LIBRARY TO TAKE ALL THESE BOOKS. THEY'D NEED TO BE DIFFERENT HEIGHTS BECAUSE THE BOOKS ARE ALL DIFFERENT SIZES.

I THOUGHT WE COULD JUST BUY MDF SHELVING AND ATTACH IT WITH ANGLE BRACKETS.

IF YOU'RE PUTTING BOOKS ON THE SHELVES, THE STRAIN WOULD BE TOO MUCH ON THE SCREWS THAT HOLD THE BRACKETS TO THE WALLS. THE DEEPER THE SHELVES, THE GREATER THE STRAIN.

WHAT DO YOU SUGGEST?

SOUNDS GREAT!

WHY NOT THINK ABOUT ADJUSTABLE SHELVING, SO YOU CAN CHANGE THE HEIGHTS OF THE SHELVES WHEN YOU WANT TO? WE HAVE A STRONG HEAVYWEIGHT SHELVING KIT IN STOCK, WHICH INCLUDES ALL THE BRACKETS AND FIXINGS.

THIS LOOKS SIMPLE. WHY DON'T YOU GO OUT SHOPPING FOR THE AFTERNOON, AND I'LL HAVE IT ALL FINISHED BY THE TIME YOU GET BACK?

Caroline is more suspicious than ever that Kevin is secretly bringing in outside help. The boyfriend she used to know could never have attempted a project like this on his own. She decides to set a little trap...

1 The Captain checks the walls for pipes and cables, then marks in pencil where he is going to attach each of the tracks. He positions the first track and checks it is vertical. He uses a pencil to mark the fixing holes, then drills into the wall, inserts a wallplug and screws the first track into position by the top screw only. (To decide on your ideal track spacing, choose the heavy load option in the handy chart on page 129.)

IF I ATTACH IT WITH THE TOP SCREW FIRST, CHECK THAT THE TRACK IS VERTICAL AND MARK THE OTHER SCREW HOLES, THEN I CAN JUST SWING THE TRACK TO ONE SIDE WHILE I DRILL AND PLUG THE REST OF THE HOLES.

2 Rest a spirit level on top of the first track so its other end reaches the vertical mark for the second track position. Make a horizontal mark across the vertical one to indicate where the top of the second track will go. Fix it as before.

3 Attach the brackets to the two tracks, position the shelves and screw the brackets to the shelves.

IF YOU DON'T TAKE CARE AT THIS STAGE, YOU'LL FIND THAT YOUR SHELVES DON'T FIT AT ALL THE DIFFERENT LEVELS — WHICH IS THE WHOLE POINT OF ADJUSTABLE SHELVING.

4 If you want your shelves flush against the wall, you'll have to cut out notches to fit around the tracks. Mark the shape, make two saw cuts, then use a chisel and hammer to cut out the notch. Check the fit of the shelves, adjusting the notches if necessary before fixing the shelves in place.

Suddenly Captain Competent hears a floorboard creak in the hall and he realizes that Caroline has come home early. He flings off the toolbelt just in the nick of time.

I HEARD ANOTHER VOICE IN THE ROOM. IT WAS MUCH DEEPER THAN YOURS. DO YOU HAVE A HELPER, KEVIN? OWN UP! THE GAME'S OVER.

NO, HONESTLY, PUMPKIN. I'VE JUST HAD A BIT OF A COLD LATELY... AND I ALWAYS TALK TO MYSELF WHILE I'M WORKING.

I HOPE YOU'RE NOT LYING TO ME, KEVIN. I DON'T LIKE BEING LIED TO. AND ONE OTHER THING — I HATE BEING CALLED PUMPKIN.

CHAPTER 4 PRESENTS...

CAPTAIN COMPETENT'S
DECORATING

Painting is the **DIY** job most people feel confident enough to attempt themselves. 'How hard can it be?' they think. Excuse me while I chortle up my sleeve. In this chapter, you'll get all the basic advice you should need to paint, wallpaper or tile any room in the house, plus warnings about some of the most common pitfalls ... but if you're anything like our friend Kevin, you'll invent some new ones of your own.

WHEREVER I GO, MY ADORING PUBLIC GAZE LONGINGLY AT MY FABULOUS PHYSIQUE, BUT I TRY NOT TO LET IT FAZE ME.

WHICH PAINT?

It's not just the colour you have to worry about when buying paint – there are loads of different types as well. For large areas like walls and ceilings, choose from a water-based emulsion paint in a matt finish, which is good for disguising uneven surfaces; silk-finish, which is hard-wearing and can be wiped clean in the event of spillages; or satin finish, which is half-way between matt and silk. Buy good-quality paint rather than the one that is going cheap on a market stall – you'll need fewer coats so it will go farther.

If you're painting bare wood or plaster, you'll need a primer first to provide a good base. Most emulsions need two coats for good coverage, but you can also buy one-coat emulsions which – believe it or not – just need one coat. While we're talking about emulsions, opt for anti-condensation types for kitchens and bathrooms, which are moisture- and grease-resistant and can be scrubbed down if they get grubby. And if your walls are particularly bumpy and cracked, textured paints are much thicker and cover flaws better.

Acrylic paints are more versatile and can often be used for wood and metal as well as walls. They are available in matt, satin and gloss finishes. Gloss paints look good on woodwork, and the solvent-based types are hardest-wearing – but the downside is that solvent-based paints need to be applied over an undercoat and they give off nasty smelly fumes while you're working with them.

Is that clear? Now all you need to do is calculate the area you want to cover and check on the side of the paint can to see how much coverage it offers. As a very rough rule of thumb, you might cover from 9 to 15 sq m (11 to 18 sq yd) with a 1 litre can of paint.

WHICH PAPER?

For professional results, always put up lining paper first if your walls are cracked or uneven (see pages 150–1). Standard wallpapers are flat with a design machine-printed on them; avoid the cheapest ones, which will tear easily. Paste-the-wall papers are quick and easy to hang, without the fiddle and mess of lifting long strips of pasted paper – as the name suggests, you paste the wall instead. You can get embossed or flock wallpapers with a raised pattern, which are more expensive, or even specialist hand-printed ones with exclusive designs. Choose water-resistant vinyl papers for kitchens and bathrooms, and avoid woodchip papers at all costs – unless you want to demonstrate your bad taste to all and sundry.

WHICH TILES?

STANDARD CERAMIC WALL TILES

Wall tiles come in a range of different sizes and shapes. Rectangles and squares are the most popular and widely available. You can also buy them with rounded edges to fit on sills and the sides of counter tops, although these are harder to find. Mosaic tiles are tiny squares that are usually sold in sheets with mesh backing. You can buy plain colours, marble-effect finishes or highly patterned, decorative tiles for borders and inserts.

FLOOR TILES

Floor tiles are available in a wide range of materials, from vinyl to ceramic, cork to carpet. The sizes are often larger than those of wall tiles, but many of the principles for laying them out are the same (*see page 166*).

HOW MANY WILL YOU NEED?

When deciding how many tiles to buy, measure the area of the surface to be tiled, allowing for any alcoves and bays, and make your calculations based on the size of your tiles. It helps to draw a plan on squared paper. Always buy several extra in case you accidentally break or damage some, either when fitting them or at a later date.

Calculate the perimeter of the room you want to paper and the height of your ceiling. Then consult the chart below to see how many rolls of standard paper you would need. Buy extra if you're choosing a paper with a large repeat pattern, as there will be much more wastage as you match up the pattern at the edge of each strip.

When you buy several rolls of paper, make sure each has the same batch number on the label. Even the smallest manufacturing variations can look obvious when the paper is hung in a room.

WALLPAPER: HOW MANY ROLLS?

HEIGHT OF CEILING	PERIMETER OF ROOM				
	10 m (33 ft)	12 m (39 ft)	14 m (46 ft)	16 m (52 ft)	20 m (66 ft)
2.1 m (7 ft)	5	5	6	7	9
2.4 m (8 ft)	5	6	7	8	10
2.6 m (8 ft 6 in)	5	6	7	9	11
2.8 m (9 ft)	5	6	7	9	11
3 m (9 ft 6 in)	6	7	8	9	12

PREPARE TO STRIP

GETTING YOUR WALLS AND WOODWORK READY

NOW, FLUFFY, WHAT'S IT TO BE? ARE YOU GOING TO GO OUT FOR THE DAY OR DO YOU WANT ME TO COVER YOU WITH A DUST SHEET?

1 Before you begin any decorating job, cover the floors and furniture with dust sheets. Remove shelves and fixings from walls. Banish any pets for the duration – the chemical fumes will be bad for them, and you don't really want cat hair on a freshly painted wall.

2 If the walls and ceiling are painted, you just need to fill any holes and cracks, scrape off any areas of peeling paint, then wash down with a sugar soap solution to remove any grease and dirt that could affect your finish. Wear gloves and goggles to stop the sugar soap irritating your skin or splashing into your eyes.

ALWAYS WASH FROM THE TOP DOWNWARDS SO THAT DIRTY WATER DOESN'T TRICKLE ON TO AREAS YOU'VE ALREADY CLEANED. CEILING FIRST, THEN WALLS AND SKIRTING BOARDS LAST. THE TOP OF THE SKIRTING BOARDS IS ALWAYS THE MUCKIEST BIT.

3 Kevin's dining room wall is covered with cork tiles – a charming decorative scheme he inherited from the previous occupant. The Captain tries to prise them off with a stripping knife, but finds that the adhesive underneath is stuck to the wall.

YUCK! THIS GLUE'S STUCK FAST. I'LL NEED MY SUPER-DUPER HOT-AIR GUN TO SOFTEN IT.

4 You can soften old dried-on adhesive with a hot-air gun, then use a stripping knife, but removing cork tiles is a slow, messy job. The adhesive used to put them up is very strong. An alternative would be to paper over them with heavy-duty lining paper.

5 To remove the delightful wallpaper in Kevin's bedroom, first of all the Captain makes holes in the paper with an orbital scorer. If you don't have one, you could use the edge of a scraper, but make sure you don't damage the plaster underneath.

6 Mix up a bucket of hot water with a little detergent and soak the wallpaper a section at a time. Let the water soak in for around five minutes, then it should come away from the wall in large strips rather than little fragments.

CAPTAIN'S TIP
It's a good idea to paint the ceiling before you remove any wallcoverings. That way, any splashes of paint won't matter.

**ALTERNATIVELY**

Instead of soaking the paper the old-fashioned way, you can work more quickly using a steam stripper — which is basically a tank filled with water that is heated till it boils and releases steam. You just hold the steaming plate against a section of wall for a minute, then use your stripping knife to peel the paper off. Steam strippers are essential if you're removing washable or painted wallpaper.

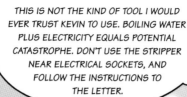

I SAID LARGE STRIPS RATHER THAN FRAGMENTS! SEEMS THE CARTOONIST IS TRYING TO MAKE ME LOOK STUPID.

THIS IS NOT THE KIND OF TOOL I WOULD EVER TRUST KEVIN TO USE. BOILING WATER PLUS ELECTRICITY EQUALS POTENTIAL CATASTROPHE. DON'T USE THE STRIPPER NEAR ELECTRICAL SOCKETS, AND FOLLOW THE INSTRUCTIONS TO THE LETTER.

CAPTAIN'S TIP
After stripping wallpaper, rub down walls with a sanding block or power sander, and fill any cracks, holes or depressions with filler (see pages 56–7).

7 If your doors and window frames have several layers of old, flaking paint that have built up over the years, you can use a hot-air gun to strip it. Direct the nozzle over a section at a time, then use a scraper to scrape off the paint from the areas you've softened up.

DON'T LET YOUR HAND GET IN FRONT OF THE NOZZLE! THAT WOULD BE VERY SILLY.

CAPTAIN'S TIP

If you live in an old house and suspect there could be lead in the paint, buy a lead testing kit to check before you strip. If there is any lead, you may need expert help to deal with it — don't risk lead poisoning.

YOU CAN ALSO BUY PASTE PAINT STRIPPERS. THESE ARE APPLIED WITH A PAINTBRUSH, LIKE THE LIQUID ONES, BUT NEED TO BE LEFT FOR A COUPLE OF HOURS TO TAKE EFFECT – AND I'M IN A HURRY TO GET ON WITH THE PAINTING.

8 Use a shave hook to remove old paint from sneaky crevices and crannies. Pull it towards you through the crevices after the paint stripper has started to work.

ALTERNATIVELY

If you don't fancy brandishing a hot-air gun, you can buy a liquid paint stripper and apply it with an old paintbrush. Wait for the paint to start bubbling, then strip it with your scraper. You might have to do this more than once if there are several layers of paint. Not the most fun part of the job.

IF THESE CHEMICALS ARE STRONG ENOUGH TO MAKE PAINT BLISTER, IMAGINE WHAT THEY COULD DO TO YOUR SKIN. BE VERY CAREFUL USING THEM AND KEEP THEM WELL OUT OF REACH OF CHILDREN, PETS AND PEOPLE CALLED KEVIN.

9 When you've finished stripping the paint, sand your doors and windows back to bare wood in order to get a neat finish.

GET INTO THE GROOVES! FOR THE FIDDLY LITTLE BITS IN WINDOW FRAMES, I USE A SANDING BLOCK.

10 After stripping and sanding your woodwork, fill any holes with wood filler, treat knots with knotting compound, then apply wood primer to provide a good base coat.

HOPE CAROLINE HAD FINISHED WITH HER STOCKING – IT'S NOT GOING TO LOOK SO ATTRACTIVE AFTER THIS TREATMENT.

11 Remember all the painting tips from pages 36–7? Stir your paint well with a clean wooden stick to blend the pigment and the medium together, then filter some through a piece of fine muslin or an old stocking into a paint kettle.

12 Prepare your tools. Professional decorators like to 'wear in' new brushes by using them to apply primer or basecoat first, but just rubbing the brush in the palm of your hand will help to shed any loose bristles. Brushes should be dry before use.

Make sure you have everything you need to hand so you are not climbing up and down ladders all day. Most people wear overalls or old clothes to paint, but of course Captain Competent never makes mistakes, so he doesn't need to cover up his stylish superhero outfit.

S'POSE I'D BETTER GET ON. KEVIN WANTS ME TO FINISH THE FIRST COAT IN THE SITTING ROOM TODAY SO HE CAN SHOW IT TO CAROLINE TONIGHT...

PAINTING CEILINGS AND WALLS...

WITHOUT PAINTING YOURSELF AS WELL

YOU LESSER BEINGS MAY NEED TO WEAR AN OLD HAT AND GOGGLES TO STOP PAINT DRIPPING IN YOUR HAIR AND EYES. MY PAINT NEVER DRIPS.

CAPTAIN'S KIT
* hat and goggles
* work platform
* long-handled roller and paint tray
* emulsion paint * paint kettle
* screwdriver * cutting-in brush
* 50 mm (2 in) paintbrush
* paint shield
* paint pad or 150 mm (6 in) brush
* long-handled mini roller * corner roller

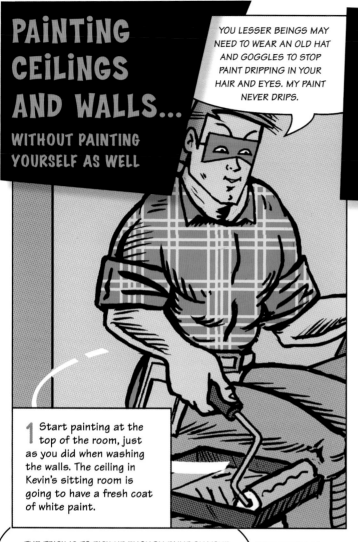

1 Start painting at the top of the room, just as you did when washing the walls. The ceiling in Kevin's sitting room is going to have a fresh coat of white paint.

2 You should work in strips along the ceiling, moving away from the main light source in the room — probably the largest window. Dip the roller in your paint tray, roll it backwards and forwards over the ridges, and start your first row, but leave a gap around the edges of the ceiling for now.

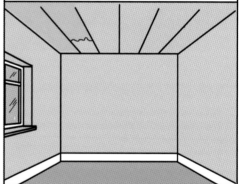

THE TRICK IS TO PICK UP ENOUGH PAINT ON YOUR ROLLER SO THAT IT GIVES YOU NICE EVEN COVERAGE, BUT NOT SO MUCH THAT IT SPLATTERS ALL OVER THE PLACE, LIKE THE TIME KEVIN ACCIDENTALLY SPRAY-PAINTED POOR FLUFFY.

3 Load your roller and start the second strip of paint, cutting into the previous one while the edge is still wet. See page 37 for more advice on rolling.

4 When you reach a plaster ceiling rose or light fitting, you will get the neatest effect if you unscrew it or remove it and paint underneath. Switch off the electricity at the consumer unit first, just in case. If the rose is difficult to remove, just paint around it carefully using a cutting-in brush with a slanted edge to butt up as close as possible.

I DON'T BELIEVE IN HIDING MY LIGHT UNDER A BUSHEL. NO SIRREE!

5 When you've finished applying the first coat over the main part of the ceiling, it's time to go back and fill in the edges. Use a small paintbrush, no more than 50 mm (2 in) wide, to blend the paint right to the edges where the ceiling meets the walls. The Captain is using a paint shield to protect Kevin's new coving as he paints up to it. (If you're planning to fit new coving, it will be easier to paint the room first, then stick the coving up later.)

SOME PEOPLE PREFER TO DO THE EDGES FIRST, THEN FILL IN THE CENTRE. IT DOESN'T MATTER, SO LONG AS YOU WORK QUICKLY ENOUGH TO CUT IN WHILE THE PAINT IS STILL WET.

6 If you don't plan to use coving, but you are going to paint the walls after you've done the ceiling, then bring a thin strip of ceiling paint down around the top of the walls. You can paint over it later, which will give you a nice neat edge.

7 No one ever manages to paint a ceiling without getting a crick in their neck. That's why it's best to use a roller so that you can finish each coat as quickly as possible.

I'VE GOT NEW RESPECT FOR THAT MICHELANGELO FELLOW. HOW ON EARTH DID HE EVER HOLD HIS HEAD UP AGAIN AFTER FIVE YEARS PAINTING THE CEILING OF THE SISTINE CHAPEL?

8 Bad news, Captain. You'll have to let this coat dry, apply the second coat and let it dry as well before you can start painting the walls. Why don't you do the dining room and bedroom ceilings while you're waiting? (It's a good idea to plan your work so that you can leave a room to dry overnight, then work on it again next morning.)

CONTINUED OVER

9 To paint a wall, start at the top – in the right-hand corner if you're right-handed and in the left-hand corner if you're left-handed. Use a 50 mm (2 in) brush with a paint shield to work up to the edge of the coving (or the edge of the ceiling). Alternatively, read the section on beading on page 37.

CAPTAIN'S TIP
Don't use gloss paint on walls or ceilings, or you'll highlight bumps and irregularities in the plasterwork.

ALTERNATIVELY

If you prefer, you can use a paint pad, but make sure you coat your pad well for even coverage. Work in strips about four times the width of your pad and keep moving it up and down (see page 36).

ALTERNATIVELY

If you like working with paintbrushes, use a 150 mm (6 in) brush to cover the main part of the wall and work in blocks of around 1 sq m (1 sq yd) at a time, blending the edges.

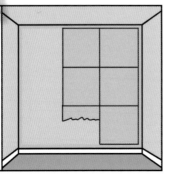

10 When you've filled in the top edge with a brush, the fastest way to cover a large wall is with a roller. Work in horizontal bands that are roughly 610 mm (24 in) wide, moving from top to bottom and blending in wet edges.

ONLY TAKE TEA BREAKS WHEN YOU'VE FINISHED A WALL. IF YOU HAVEN'T BLENDED IN ALL YOUR WET EDGES, YOU MIGHT FIND THE JUNCTIONS SHOW.

CAPTAIN'S TIP
Choose a roller with a short pile for smooth walls, and a shaggier pile for textured surfaces.

11 Use a long-handled mini roller to paint behind radiators. If you get any paint on the metal, wipe it off with a damp cloth before it dries.

12 When you reach a corner where the next wall will be painted in the same colour, you can use a cutting-in brush or corner roller to get paint right into the angle. If the adjoining wall is to be a different colour, you could apply masking tape along the edge of the unpainted one to protect it, or use the beading technique (*see page 37*) if you have a steady hand.

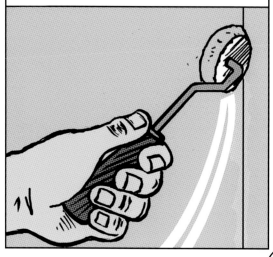

13 If your skirting is going to be painted later, you don't need to worry about slight overlaps. However, if it's already finished, like Kevin's, use a paint shield to protect it as you work your way along the border with a small brush.

see page 37

CAPTAIN'S TIP
Solvent-based gloss paints make a hard-wearing finish for skirting, helping to protect it from bumps and scuffs, but should never be applied to expanded-polystyrene coving, where it would be a major fire risk.

14 Caroline had said she would come around at about six o'clock to see how her boyfriend was getting on. The Captain suspects she will arrive early to try to catch him out, so at half-past-five, he takes the toolbelt off and Kevin continues painting the wall on his own.

WELL DONE, DARLING. THE COLOUR LOOKS FABULOUS AND I CAN'T BELIEVE YOU HAVEN'T MADE A MESS!

AHEM! MAYBE YOU'LL HAVE MORE FAITH IN ME IN FUTURE.

THIS IS FUN. I ALWAYS LIKED OUR PAINTING CLASSES AT SCHOOL.

How long do you think Kevin will be able to hide his painted hand and sleeve from her?

PAINTING DOORS AND WINDOWS...

WITHOUT GETTING THEM STUCK

CAPTAIN'S KIT

* screwdriver * block of wood
* 12 mm (¹/₂ in), 25 mm (1 in) and
50 mm (2 in) brushes, as required
* acrylic or gloss paint
* cloths * masking tape * paint shield

I ALWAYS PUT THE DOOR HANDLE IN MY TOOLBELT SO I DON'T MISLAY IT. IF THE WEDGE SLIPS OUT AND THE DOOR SHUTS, YOU COULD FIND YOURSELF TRAPPED IN THE ROOM.

1 Before painting a door, unscrew the handles with a screwdriver and wedge the door open with a block of wood. Make sure it doesn't move.

2 You'll find it easier and get a better finish if you paint panelled doors in a particular sequence. Pick up wet edges before they dry and always paint in the direction of the grain of the wood.

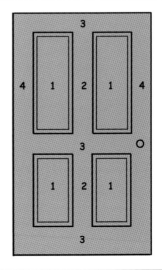

3 Use a cutting-in brush to paint the edges of the panels and mouldings first. Don't overload your brush – it looks horrible if dribbles of paint dry in the mouldings.

IF YOUR BRUSH SHEDS ANY BRISTLES, PICK THEM UP WITH A CLOTH AS YOU GO ALONG SO YOUR DOOR DOESN'T LOOK LIKE AN OLD MAN'S CHIN.

4 Paint the large panels (numbered 1 in the diagram), followed by the vertical bit down the middle (2). Continue with the top, centre and bottom horizontal rails (3), then the verticals at the sides (4).

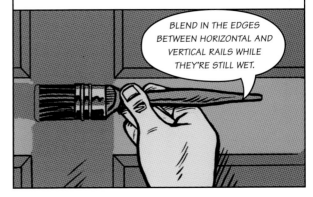

BLEND IN THE EDGES BETWEEN HORIZONTAL AND VERTICAL RAILS WHILE THEY'RE STILL WET.

5 The rule is that you paint the latch side of the door in the same colour as the opening face – in this case, blue. The hinged edge should be the same colour as the closing face.

OF COURSE, I'M NORMALLY A CHEERFUL OLD SUPERHERO WHEN IT COMES TO PAINTING, BUT I'M FEELING A LITTLE BLUE TODAY. HA, HA.

6 Kevin's bedroom has a flush door rather than a panelled one. This is much more straightforward to paint. Just imagine it divided into 8 blocks and work from top to bottom, right to left (if you're right-handed) or left to right (if you're left-handed). Cover up that purple!

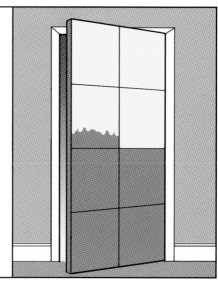

7 When you're painting glass doors, the sequence is similar to panelled – but without the panels! Stick masking tape on the glass to protect it.

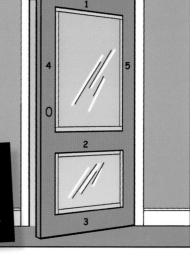

CAPTAIN'S TIP
If you're using a solvent-based gloss paint, make sure there is plenty of ventilation in the room or the fumes could make you feel woozy.

8 Sash windows are a bit tricky because you have to avoid sticking the two sashes together – unless you are happy to leave your windows permanently open. You can use a paint shield to protect the glass, or stick masking tape around the edges, but leave a gap of about 3mm (⅛ in) and let the paint extend on to the glass, covering the edges of the putty to seal them.

SEE THE NEXT PAGE TO FIND OUT THE ORDER IN WHICH I PAINT THE PARTS OF THIS WINDOW. IF YOU DON'T FOLLOW IT EXACTLY, YOU'LL END UP WITH BITS YOU CAN'T REACH IN THE MIDDLE.

9 Raise the bottom sash and lower the top one, so that you can paint the lower horizontal rail of the top sash first. Paint the vertical rails above it as far as you can reach. And don't forget the underside of the lower rail.

THE BOTTOM SASH SITS IN FRONT OF THE TOP SASH WHEN YOU'RE INSIDE THE ROOM. OF COURSE, IT'S THE OTHER WAY AROUND FROM THE OUTSIDE. BUT WE'RE NOT PAINTING EXTERIORS TODAY.

10 Raise the top sash so it is almost closed, leaving a gap of around 25 mm (1 in). Lower the bottom sash to the almost closed position. You should now be able to paint the rest of the top sash.

CAPTAIN'S TIP

Painting windows always takes longer than you think because of all the tricky little bits and pieces. Do them early in the day so they have time to dry and you don't have to leave your windows open overnight.

12 Paint around the outer frame of the window and along the window sill.

OF COURSE, IT'S TAKING ME A LONG TIME TO WRITE THEM, BECAUSE THERE'S SO MUCH TO SAY. THE WORLD WILL HAVE TO WAIT.

11 Now paint the bottom sash, including the underside of the bottom cross-rail.

DID I MENTION THAT I'M WRITING MY MEMOIRS? THEY COVER EVERYTHING FROM WHEN I WAS A TWINKLE IN MY SUPERHERO PARENTS' EYES. A BLINDINGLY BRIGHT TWINKLE, OF COURSE.

13 Wait until the paint on the sashes is touch-dry before applying a thin coat of paint to the frame sides. Make sure you keep the sash cords well out of the way because they can break, fray or become stuck if they get paint on them.

14 If you're painting casement windows, it's best to remove the window handles and stays first, and use a couple of screws and a piece of wire to hold the windows open while the new paint dries.

ONCE THE FRAME SIDES ARE DRY, CHECK THAT THE SASHES STILL RUN AND THE WINDOWS OPEN AND CLOSE EASILY. YOU MAY HAVE TO GIVE THEM A BIT OF A TUG AT FIRST AND SAY 'OPEN, SESAME'.

16 Finally – you know what's coming next – clear up and clean all your brushes, rollers and tools, following the techniques described on page 21.

15 Follow the painting sequence: first the horizontal bar, then top and bottom cross-rails, followed by the vertical rails, edges, frame and window sill.

CROSS LINING
A HAPPY SURFACE FOR YOUR WALLPAPER TO STICK TO

CAPTAIN'S KIT
* lining paper
* wallpaper paste
* paste brush
* wallpaper scissors
* stepladder
* paperhanging brush
* spirit level
* straightedge
* pencil
* tape measure
* pasting table

1 All the downstairs ceilings, walls, doors and window frames have been painted, so now Kevin turns his attention upstairs to the bedroom.

THE OLD MAN IN THE DIY SHOP TOLD ME TO HANG LINING PAPER TO PROVIDE A GOOD SURFACE FOR WALLPAPER, BUT IT ALL LOOKS A BIT DAUNTING. I THINK I'LL JUST SLIP ON MY TOOLBELT.

2 After stripping the old wallpaper, start from a top corner and use a pencil, spirit level and straightedge to mark hanging positions for your lining paper. You can either go around the room horizontally, working your way down length by length or, if you're not experienced at paper hanging, you'll find it easier to hang lining paper vertically – see the Captain's Tip.

CAPTAIN'S TIP
If you are hanging lining paper vertically, make sure the seams don't fall in the same places as the wallpaper seams. Decide where you'll hang the first length of wallpaper, then put up half a width of lining paper, so the seams are staggered.

I'VE MIXED UP MY PASTE ALREADY. IT'S BEST TO LET IT SETTLE FOR A WHILE BEFORE USE.

3 Cut the first length of paper and lay it flat on the pasting table.

4 Place weights on the ends of the paper to stop them curling up, if necessary. Some paper will probably hang over the end of the table. Pick up some paste on your brush, wipe off the excess, then brush the paste down the centre of the paper and out in slanting strokes towards the edges. Push the length to the far edge of the table and paste to the edge of the paper, then draw it to the near edge of the table and paste to that edge. Keep pasting until your paper is nicely tacky all over.

5 Fold the pasted paper over on itself and move it along the table if you need to paste an overhanging part. When all of the paper is pasted, fold it over on itself a few times to form loose concertina pleats that you can lift easily to hang on the wall. Don't press down, though, or they'll stick together.

WITH SOME PAPERS, THE MANUFACTURERS RECOMMEND LETTING THE PASTE SOAK IN FOR A WHILE BEFORE HANGING. READ THE INSTRUCTIONS ON THE PACK!

6 Lift the first length on to the wall, carefully aligning it with your pencil marks. Unfold the concertina bit by bit and smooth your lining paper downwards with a paperhanger's brush to remove any trapped air.

WE WALLPAPER EXPERTS HATE TRAPPED AIR BUBBLES. THEY GIVE ME HICCUPS.

7 Paste the second length and hang it with the edge butting up to the first. Keep hanging successive lengths until you've covered the walls. Cut off the excess with wallpaper scissors and brush it down neatly.

8 When you reach corners, don't run the lining paper around them on to adjoining walls, or allow any overlaps. Trim the excess so the paper tucks neatly into the corners. Do the same at doors and windows.

YOU'LL DEAL WITH CORNERS DIFFERENTLY WHEN IT'S REAL WALLPAPER. READ ON!

9 Let the lining paper dry for at least 12 hours before you hang the wallpaper on top. This doesn't mean you can have a rest, though, Captain Competent. Don't forget that Kevin wants you to paper the stairwell too, so you'd better get on with lining it first.

JUST WHEN I THOUGHT I HAD A LITTLE TIME TO REST ON MY LAURELS...

HANGING PAPER...
WITHOUT IT DRIVING YOU UP THE WALL

IF THERE'S A BIG FEATURE IN THE ROOM, SUCH AS A FIREPLACE, HANG THE FIRST DROP DEAD CENTRE ABOVE IT TO GIVE A SYMMETRICAL LOOK.

1 Start on a wall that has no obstructions and work away from the room's main light source. Leave a 25 mm (1 in) overlap to go around the first corner, then measure and use a plumbline to mark a vertical pencil line where the edge of the first drop will fall.

2 Measure the height of the wall and add 100 mm (4 in) to allow for trimming at the top and bottom, then cut the first length of paper. With the pattern side up, hold the roll against the first cut length to match the pattern, then cut the second length. Do the same for the remainder of the wall, and number your pieces on the back top left corner.

I MEASURE THE HEIGHT OF THE WALL FOR EVERY DROP. CEILING HEIGHTS CAN CHANGE FROM ONE END OF A WALL TO ANOTHER. DON'T BLAME THE BUILDERS – HOUSES OFTEN MOVE IN MYSTERIOUS WAYS.

3 Paste the first drop of wallpaper just as you did for the lining paper, then fold it into a loose concertina. Starting at the top of the wall, position the right-hand edge against the pencil line on the wall and let the left-hand edge curl around the corner. Leave 50 mm (2 in) overlapping the ceiling or coving, which you will trim later.

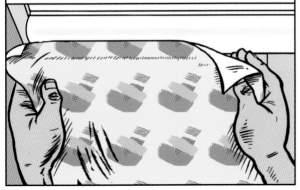

IT MAY SOUND OBVIOUS, BUT WITH PATTERNED WALLPAPERS ALWAYS CHECK WHICH WAY UP THE PATTERN GOES. DECORATORS HAVE COME A CROPPER WITH THIS IN THE PAST. WHO, ME? NEVER!

4 Use a paperhanger's brush to smooth the first drop into position, working downwards to remove any air bubbles. Don't let your paper drop, as it could tear – lower it gradually, unfolding the concertina as you go. When you reach the skirting board, let the excess overhang it.

5 Run the blunt edge of your scissors along the top edge to make a crease where the paper overlaps the ceiling or coving. Gently pull the top of the paper away from the wall, cut along the crease, then smooth the paper back down again. Do the same at the bottom along the skirting board.

WIPE UP ANY PASTE THAT OOZES OUT AS YOU GO ALONG, AND WIPE THE COVING AND SKIRTING CLEAN BEFORE THE PASTE DRIES ON THEM.

6 Hang the second length, butting it up to the edge of the first and matching the pattern. Once you've hung a few lengths, go back and press down the seams with a seam roller.

DON'T USE THE SEAM ROLLER IF THERE'S A RAISED OR EMBOSSED PATTERN ON YOUR PAPER. OTHERWISE, YOU'LL FLATTEN IT – MIGHT AS WELL CALL IT A STEAM ROLLER!

7 When you reach the first internal corner, measure the distance from the edge of the last drop to the corner, add 25 mm (1 in) and cut the next length of paper to that width. Save the bit you trim off.

25 MM (1 IN)

8 Paste the paper and hang it, butting its left edge against the last drop and with a 25 mm (1 in) overlap going around the corner on to the adjoining wall. You may need to snip little cuts in the overlapping bit to get it to lie flat. Run a seam roller over the overlap.

WITH VINYL WALLPAPERS, YOU HAVE TO PUT SPECIAL VINYL ADHESIVE ON THE OVERLAP SO IT WILL STICK TO ITSELF.

9 Measure the width of the piece you trimmed off, then plumb a vertical line that distance away from the corner. Paste the narrow piece and hang it over the top of the overlapping bit, aligning it with your pencil line on the right and matching the pattern as closely as you can.

KEEP USING YOUR PLUMBLINE, OR YOU'LL FIND YOU'RE GOING OFF AT A TANGENT!

10 Some rooms have external corners as well, perhaps where there are alcoves or bays. They are treated in a similar way to internal corners – hang a width that allows a 25 mm (1 in) strip to bend around the corner – but it will look neater if you butt the next length up to the bit that's run around rather than sticking it on top.

THIS JOB IS DRIVING ME ROUND THE BEND.

11 When you reach a door frame, hang the last full drop of paper up to the frame and let it sit loosely over the door. Smooth it on to the wall with a paperhanger's brush to get rid of air bubbles, then make a diagonal cut through the excess paper at the top corner of the frame.

WHEN IS A DOOR NOT A DOOR? WHEN IT'S AJAR. A JAR! GET IT?

12 Press down above the top of the door frame to crease the paper, then peel back and trim the excess paper. Brush the paper into the sides of the door frame, then trim off the excess there.

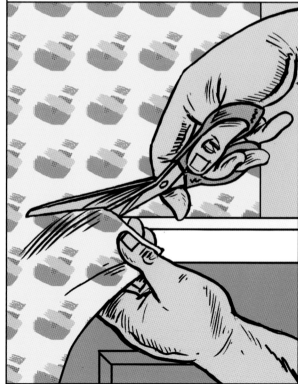

13 Hang the short drop over the top of the door and trim it to fit. Hang your next length on the other side of the door, making sure you match the pattern, and trim as in step 11.

THIS WOULD NOT BE A GREAT MOMENT FOR ANYONE TO TRY TO OPEN THE DOOR.

14 Treat windows with architraves in the same way as doors, but note that window recesses can be slightly trickier. Cut and hang a length that goes up to and over the recess. Make a horizontal cut along the top edge of the recess to the corner, then use a brush to smooth the paper into the recess. Press it in firmly and trim off the excess.

CAPTAIN'S TIP
Wipe your pasting table and clean wallpaper scissors if any paste gets onto them.

15 You'll notice that there's a gap along the top of the recess. Measure and cut a strip of paper to cover this, allowing a 25 mm (1 in) overlap that will curve up on to the wall above the recess. You may need a couple of strips to reach the other side.

KEEP MATCHING YOUR PATTERN AS CLOSELY AS YOU CAN, OR IT WILL ALL LOOK A BIT SKEW-WHIFF!

16 Lift the paper above the recess, slip your overlap underneath it, then smooth it down neatly.

TEAR THE OVERLAP BY HAND, SO AN OBVIOUS STRAIGHT SEAM DOESN'T SHOW THROUGH.

ONCE YOU GET PAST AN OBSTRUCTION, YOU MIGHT FIND YOU'VE GONE A BIT SQUINT. USE YOUR PLUMBLINE TO SET YOU BACK ON THE STRAIGHT AND NARROW.

17 Repeat the process on the other side of the recess and paper beneath the window itself, if required. Then, as they say in the movies, it's a wrap!

18 Another type of obstruction that you'll have to negotiate are light switches and wall sockets. You'll get the neatest finish if you switch off the electricity at the mains and partially unscrew the faceplates so that you can tuck the paper under them a fraction. Hang your drop of paper over the faceplate and smooth it down, pressing it lightly against the socket or switch.

PRESS THE PAPER AGAINST YOUR SWITCH JUST ENOUGH TO MAKE AN IMPRESSION, BUT NOT ENOUGH TO TEAR IT.

19 Snip diagonal cuts from the centre of the faceplate out to each of the four corners. Trim off the triangle shapes.

IF YOUR LIGHT SWITCHES OR SOCKETS ARE CIRCULAR, YOU'LL NEED TO MAKE SEVERAL CUTS IN A KIND OF STAR SHAPE IN ORDER TO EASE THE PAPER AROUND THEM.

20 If you've taken down shelves and pictures, it's a good idea to mark the fixing holes with small bits of matchstick (remove the match heads first, or they'll stain your paper). Hang the wallpaper over the top, ease the matchsticks through gently, without tearing the paper, then smooth it all down.

21 When you want to replace the shelves or pictures, you can simply remove the matchsticks and insert your screws or nails directly into the old fixing holes.

SHE'S FAR TOO GOOD FOR HIM, THAT GIRL. MAYBE SHE'D LIKE TO GO OUT WITH ME INSTEAD? HMMM...

22 Another little wallpapering challenge can be papering around radiators. In fact, you only need to paper the top 150 mm (6 in) or so behind the radiator, just down to the fixing brackets, and add a strip at the bottom if it will be visible. First of all, hang a drop of paper from the ceiling and let it sit on top of the radiator.

MAKE SURE YOUR HEATING IS OFF WHILE YOU'RE DOING THIS SO YOU DON'T BURN YOURSELF. THINK THIS TIP'S TOO OBVIOUS? YOU'D BE SURPRISED.

23 Mark the rough position of the fixing brackets on the overhanging paper, cut just above them, then smooth the paper down behind the radiator with a long-handled mini roller (sometimes known helpfully as a radiator roller).

24 Cut strips to fit the area beneath the radiator and roll them into place with the mini roller.

IF THE RADIATOR REACHES RIGHT DOWN TO SKIRTING LEVEL, YOU DON'T NEED TO BOTHER WITH THIS STEP.

I'M NOT SURE ABOUT THIS PAPER – IT'S A BIT TOO SUBTLE FOR MY TASTE. ANYWAY, NO REST FOR THE WICKED – I'VE GOT TO DO THE STAIRWELL NOW.

THE HEIGHTS OF SUCCESS

PAPERING A STAIRWELL

CAPTAIN'S KIT

* stepladder, ladder and sturdy boards, plus ropes OR an adjustable work platform
* wallpaper
* wallpaper paste
* paste brush
* wallpaper scissors
* paperhanger's brush
* plumbline
* pencil
* tape measure
* pasting table
* seam roller

1 Papering a stairwell is not as tricky as you might think. The main problem is getting access to work at heights, so you need to set up a secure kind of work platform with adjustable legs. You might be able to hire one from your local DIY store, but if not...

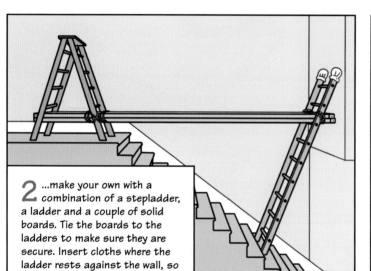

2 ...make your own with a combination of a stepladder, a ladder and a couple of solid boards. Tie the boards to the ladders to make sure they are secure. Insert cloths where the ladder rests against the wall, so it doesn't damage the plaster.

3 It's best to hang the longest drop first. Use a plumbline to mark the position in pencil at the tallest part of the stairwell, then measure it.

MAKE SURE YOUR BOARDS ARE HORIZONTAL, OR YOU'LL FEEL LIKE A CIRCUS PERFORMER.

4 Cut your first length of wallpaper. Paste and fold the paper concertina style, being careful not to tear it, then climb on to your work platform and position the top of the first length against your pencil line. Let it overlap the junction with the ceiling by 25 mm (1 in). Smooth it downwards with a paperhanger's brush.

I CAN SEE I'M GOING TO BE JUMPING ON AND OFF MY PLATFORM ALL AFTERNOON.

CAPTAIN'S TIP

Don't use complex patterned paper on stairs. You'll give yourself a massive headache trying to match the patterns on such long lengths.

5 It helps if you have someone down below who can hang the lower section. Otherwise, you'll have to balance the lower half of the concertina on your work platform...

LENGTH 1
(TOP)

6 ...climb off the platform, pull the concertina down behind it and paste the lower section of the first length down to the skirting below. Trim it diagonally to fit.

LENGTH 1
(BOTTOM)

TRY NOT TO GET PASTE ON YOUR CARPET OR FLOORING. IT'S NOT A PRETTY SIGHT!

7 Using a plumbline, mark the vertical position guide for the second length, working back up towards the landing. Cut and paste it in the same way as you did for the first length.

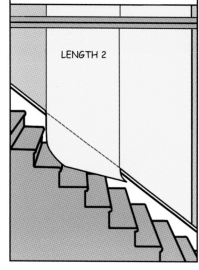

LENGTH 2

8 When you've papered up to the landing, move around to the head wall. Cut the lengths you will need to cover it, then hang the tops of each drop above the place where your ladder is resting.

HEAD WALL

9 Climb down, move the stepladder down to the hall and rest the other ends of your boards on a step that is the appropriate height. Unfold the wallpaper drops to cover the bottom of the head wall.

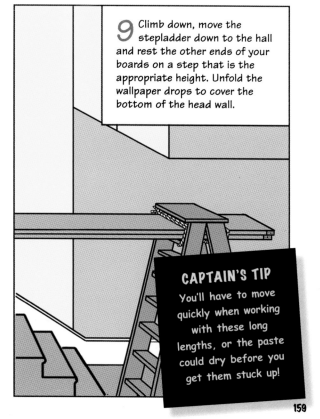

CAPTAIN'S TIP
You'll have to move quickly when working with these long lengths, or the paste could dry before you get them stuck up!

GETTING READY FOR A NIGHT ON THE TILES

CRUMBLING CRETINS! HOW DID KEVIN MANAGE TO GET THESE TILES QUITE SO SPECTACULARLY WONKY, YET STILL STICK THEM DOWN SO HARD? HOW I WISH I WAS ONE OF THOSE SUPERHEROES WHO CAN ZAP THINGS WITH LASER BEAMS.

1 The next room requiring DIY attention is Kevin's bathroom and its infamous slanting tiles. In some cases, it's possible to tile on top of old tiles – but not these! The Captain gets them off the wall by scraping out the grout, drilling into the face of the first tile, then chipping them out with a hammer and bolster chisel. Shards of tile are flying everywhere, so he's wearing his protective gear – and grumbling a lot.

2 The tiles need to sit on a level surface, so sand back any bumps and fill any holes. Note that if you need to apply a layer of filling plaster to very uneven walls, you will have to leave it to dry for about 48 hours before tiling on top.

I SUPPOSE YOU'VE GOT TO TAKE THE ROUGH WITH THE SMOOTH IN THIS LIFE.

3 Bare plaster can be porous, so prime it with a diluted solution of PVA adhesive to stop it absorbing moisture and to give a good base for the new tiles.

4 It can be useful to make a tile gauge to help plan the layout of your tiles. Take one of your wooden battens and lay it on the floor. Arrange a row of tiles along the edge, starting at one end and including the plastic spacers between tiles. Now mark the positions of all the tiles and the gaps between them in pencil on your batten. Number the tile positions, from left to right, so you can see at a glance how many tiles you need for a row just by holding your gauge against the wall.

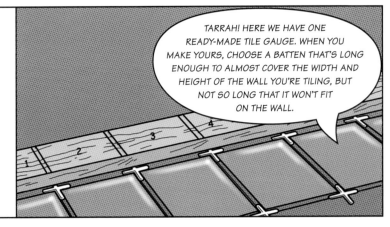

TARRAH! HERE WE HAVE ONE READY-MADE TILE GAUGE. WHEN YOU MAKE YOURS, CHOOSE A BATTEN THAT'S LONG ENOUGH TO ALMOST COVER THE WIDTH AND HEIGHT OF THE WALL YOU'RE TILING, BUT NOT SO LONG THAT IT WON'T FIT ON THE WALL.

5 It's best to start planning your tiling in the centre of the wall and work outwards. Measure and mark the central position, then hold your tile gauge vertically beside it to see how many tiles would fit above and below. If this starting position would leave you with a very narrow strip to fill at the top or bottom of the wall, move your central position down by half a tile space.

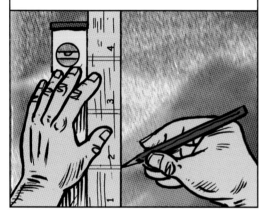

6 Do the same to plan your horizontal rows, adjusting to left or right to avoid narrow gaps at the ends of walls.

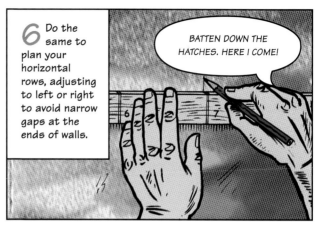

BATTEN DOWN THE HATCHES. HERE I COME!

7 Use a spirit level held against your batten to draw horizontal and vertical guidelines for all the 'field tiles' – the ones that don't need to be cut to fit at edges. Nail wooden battens up one side and along the bottom of the area to be covered by field tiles. Don't forget to check the wall with your pipe and cable detector first, and use your spirit level to make sure the battens are perfectly horizontal and vertical.

LEAVE THE NAIL HEADS PROTRUDING WHEN YOU NAIL YOUR BATTENS IN PLACE, SO THEY'RE EASY TO REMOVE AGAIN.

8 If you are tiling a wall with obstructions on it, like a sink, a window, or pipes behind lavatories, it is best to plan your tiling on paper first to make the most efficient use of your tiles. Try to make sure that two tiles meet where you need to cut around a pipe – that way you can just nip semi-circles out of each one and slide them around the pipe. If you're tiling around a window, it looks best if the tiles are centred, so plan from the window outwards.

PLAN FIRST, CUT LATER. THAT'S WHAT MY BARBER ALWAYS SAYS.

SUPER-DUPER. NOW I'M READY TO GET STICKING.

STICK 'EM UP!
TILING THE BATHROOM WALLS

> DON'T SPREAD TOO MUCH ADHESIVE, OR IT WILL START TO DRY BEFORE YOU HAVE TIME TO SET THE TILES ON IT.

1 The first field tiles will be placed in the corner between the battens. Apply adhesive to an area of about 1 sq m (1 sq yd), using the notched spreader to form neat horizontal ridges.

2 Set your first tile on the wall, pressing it firmly against the wooden battens. Position the tile above it, then the one next to it and insert plastic spacers between them.

> NEVER SLIDE A TILE INTO PLACE, OR YOU'LL END UP WITH MORE ADHESIVE AT ONE SIDE THAN THE OTHER. PLACE IT SQUARELY ON THE WALL.

3 Set the rest of the field tiles, working in blocks of roughly 1 sq m (1 sq yd) at a time, from the bottom to the top. Every couple of rows, sit a spirit level on top to check that you're not going off true.

> KEVIN, TAKE NOTE. BUBBLE IN MIDDLE IS LEVEL. BUBBLE TO SIDE IS NOT CLEVER.

4 Remove the battens. To measure edge tiles, hold a tile over the last fixed tile and butt another tile up to the wall (leaving room for grout), so its edge overlaps the whole tile. Mark the cutting line with a water-soluble pen, then cut the tile. Check the fit and adjust with a tile file. If you find this too fiddly, measure the gap to be filled at top and bottom, subtract an amount for grouting, mark those dimensions on the top and bottom edges, then join the marks to produce a cutting line.

5 There are two ways of getting a neat finish at external corners. You can stick up plastic corner trim, as the Captain is doing, using spacers to leave a gap for grouting on each side. Alternatively, you can buy round-edged tiles for corners and the edge of window sills.

> CORNER TRIM HELPS TO PROTECT THE TILES FROM CRACKING IF HEAVY OBJECTS SMASH INTO THEM. HAVE YOU EVER SEEN THE WAY KEVIN SWINGS HIS TOOLS AROUND? IT'S A SCARY SIGHT.

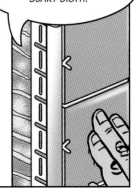

6 To tile around obtrusive bits of plumbing, make a card template (slightly bigger than the pipe to allow room for grout), then transfer the shape to a tile with water-soluble pen. Score the line freehand, nibble away the shape with pincers and file with a tile file until you achieve a good fit.

I'VE NEVER KNOWN A BATHROOM TO HAVE QUITE SO MANY PIPES!

7 Windows aren't too tricky if you've planned your tiling carefully. Just cut and fit the tiles into the different shapes required, using templates.

CURVES, CORNERS, I CAN CUT ANY OLD SHAPE YOU WANT. I COULD EVEN CARVE MY OWN ULTRA-HANDSOME PROFILE IN A TILE, IF YOU LIKE. NO?

8 If you're tiling over the top of a window recess, you'll need to pin up a wooden batten with masonry nails to support the tiles in position while the adhesive dries.

9 If you're tiling inside a window recess, you'll need to position loose wooden battens in a V shape to support the top row of tiles.

10 If you have to tile around switches or sockets, make a template (leaving space for grout) and cut your tiles to fit.

I DON'T THINK KEVIN KNOWS THIS SHAVING SOCKET IS HERE. HAVE YOU SEEN HIS CHIN LATELY?

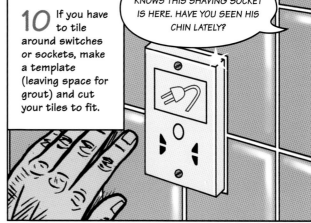

GROUT SPREADING
PLUS SOME SEALING, DRILLING AND SCREWING

1 Leave the tile adhesive to dry for the time it says on the packaging (probably around 24 hours). This means that no one can bath or shower in Kevin's bathroom for the time being.

AH, I LOVE THE SCENT OF SUPERHERO SWEAT.

2 In kitchens and bathrooms, you will need to grout tiles with waterproof grout. It's possible to buy coloured varieties instead of plain old white. Buy ready-mixed grout, or a combined adhesive-and-grout, to avoid having to mix your own. Press a small amount on to the tiles with a grout spreader and spread it upwards using diagonal strokes. Make sure that the grout is pushed firmly into the joints and over the plastic spacers.

AIM TO FILL ALL THE JOINTS UP TO THE LEVEL OF THE TILE SURFACE.

3 As soon as you've finished spreading the grout, wipe the tile surfaces clean with a damp cloth. It's much harder to remove grout once it's dried. Run a grout shaper along the joints to make them look nice and neat.

IF YOU DON'T HAVE A GROUT SHAPER, THE ROUNDED END OF A DOWEL OR A WOODEN ICE LOLLY STICK MIGHT DO THE TRICK. EAT THE LOLLY FIRST.

4 Now leave the grout to dry for the length of time the manufacturer recommends. You'll notice a white powder on the tile surface – just polish if off with a dry cloth to give a sparkling finish.

5 Remember the Old Man telling Kevin about waterproof sealant on page 94? This is going to have to be applied around the bath and the basin as well. Choose a flexible sealant for bathroom fixtures that can be prone to movement; experts recommend filling the bath with water first, so that it's heavier and the gap to be sealed is slightly wider. It helps to get a straight line if you stick a length of masking tape above and below the area and apply sealant between the two. Pull the tape off as soon as the sealant is touch dry.

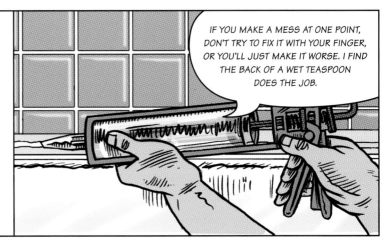

IF YOU MAKE A MESS AT ONE POINT, DON'T TRY TO FIX IT WITH YOUR FINGER, OR YOU'LL JUST MAKE IT WORSE. I FIND THE BACK OF A WET TEASPOON DOES THE JOB.

6 Now the Captain has to get down on his knees to fit Kevin's toilet-roll holder. He uses a pipe and cable detector, then marks his fixing holes. Make sure you hold the drill level and drill your fixing holes at a slow speed, using a masonry bit. If it's a large hole you need, make a smaller one first, then insert the larger drill bit.

IT WILL HELP TO STOP THE DRILL SLIPPING ON THE TILE SURFACE IF YOU APPLY A BIT OF MASKING TAPE AND DRILL THROUGH IT.

7 Insert the wallplugs and screw the toilet-roll holder into position.

MAKE SURE YOU CHOOSE A SPOT THAT'S EASY TO REACH FOR SOMEONE SITTING ON THE TOILET. OTHERWISE, THINGS CAN GET TRICKY. NUFF SAID.

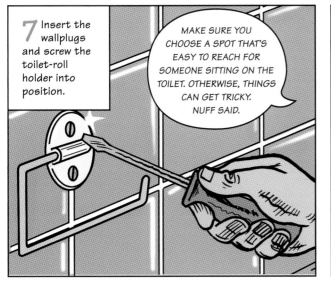

8 Kevin admires his sparkling, new, evenly tiled walls. Then he looks down at the scabby old linoleum on the floor.

WOULDN'T IT LOOK NICE IF THE FLOOR WAS TILED TO MATCH? SURELY IT CAN'T BE HARD? I'LL GET THE CAPTAIN TO DO THAT NEXT.

LAYING FLOOR TILES...
WITHOUT CRACKING UP

FLOOR TILE ADHESIVE NEEDS TO SET FOR 24 HOURS, AND YOU CAN'T WALK ON IT DURING THIS TIME. IF IT'S A ROOM YOU NEED ACCESS TO, YOU COULD TILE HALF OF IT FIRST, THEN DO THE OTHER HALF WHEN THE FIRST BIT HAS SET. KEVIN HAS DECIDED TO STAY AT HIS MUM'S UNTIL THE FLOOR'S READY.

1 The Captain rips up Kevin's lino and uses a spirit level to check the floor is level. He cleans it with detergent solution, then primes it with diluted PVA adhesive. If you are tiling over a wooden floor, create a smooth surface by laying a sheet of exterior-grade plywood over the floorboards and securing it with wood screws.

2 Measure to find the centre of your room first. You don't need to make a tile gauge, because you can just lay out the tiles to see how they fit best. Place one in the centre, then lay out from that point, remembering to insert spacers. Adjust the layout so you don't have any narrow strips at edges or awkward gaps by fittings, then draw chalk lines on the floor to show the position of the first central tile.

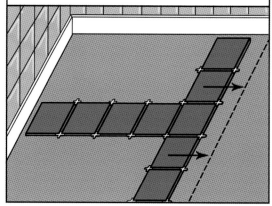

3 Start laying the whole tiles first. If you have a wooden floor, you could hammer battens down to show the outlines of the field tile area, but once the first tile is down, it will act as a positional guide. Spread tile adhesive over the first sq m (sq yd), starting at the far side of the room and working back to the door.

TAKE CARE NOT TO KNEEL IN YOUR ADHESIVE. IT DOES TERRIBLE THINGS TO SUPERHERO LYCRA LEGGINGS.

4 Position the first tile at the corner of your field, then lay the second and third ones and insert spacers between them. Bed them firmly into the adhesive to make sure there's no air trapped underneath. Work outwards from this point, spreading a sq m (sq yd) of adhesive at a time. Don't tile yourself into a corner!

KEEP USING A SPIRIT LEVEL TO MAKE SURE ALL THE TILES ARE LEVEL WITH EACH OTHER.

5 Lay out all the field tiles and leave them to set for 24 hours before coming back to do the edges. You'll need a heavy-duty tile cutter to get through thick, flooring-quality tiles. Use a chinagraph pen to mark the cutting line, leaving room for grout and a line of sealant where the edges meet bathroom fittings. Cut and position all the edging tiles, and leave them to set for 24 hours.

8 Leave the grout to harden for an hour, then polish the tiles with a soft cloth. Seal around the edges of any bathroom fittings with flexible silicone sealant.

I DON'T NEED TO TELL YOU HOW TO APPLY SEALANT AGAIN, DO I? SEE PAGE 165.

6 Use a cardboard template to trace the cutting line on tiles that have to fit around obstructions like the base of the toilet and sink pedestal.

OR BUY A FUNKY LITTLE TOOL CALLED A PROFILE GAUGE, MOULD IT AROUND YOUR OBSTRUCTION, THEN TRANSFER THE PROFILE ON TO YOUR TILE.

7 Apply the waterproof grout to the joints between tiles. Wipe it off the tile surfaces immediately. When you can see the grout beginning to set, use a grouting tool to tidy up the joints.

MAKE SURE YOUR GROUT IS FLUSH WITH THE SURFACE OF THE TILES, OR GROT WILL COLLECT IN THE HOLLOWS.

9 You should avoid giving the floor any hard use – such as Kevin clumping around on it – for another 48 hours. He is still waiting patiently at his mother's.

SO YOU KNOW HOW TO DO TILING, DO YOU? I QUITE FANCY A BIT OF TILING. I'D LIKE THOSE CORK TILES IN THE HALLWAY, NICE BLUE VINYL ONES IN THE KITCHEN, CARPET TILES IN THE SITTING ROOM... WHEN CAN YOU START?'

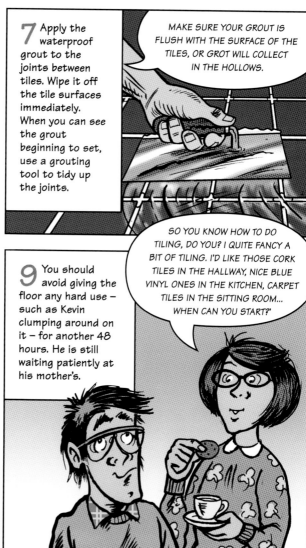

BEING FLOORED
MORE TILING CHOICES

CORK CAN BE QUITE RESILIENT IF YOU CHOOSE THE THICKEST GRADE WITH AN IMPERVIOUS SURFACE. PEOPLE OFTEN USE CORK TILES ON AN UPSTAIRS FLOOR BECAUSE THEY'RE GOOD FOR SOUNDPROOFING.

DO YOU THINK CORK WOULD BE STRONG ENOUGH FOR A HALL FLOOR? WHAT ABOUT ALL THOSE MUDDY BOOTS AND BICYCLES AND PEOPLE TRAMPING THROUGH?

DOES IT COME WITH SPACERS? AND DO YOU NEED A SPECIAL KIND OF GROUT?'

ERM, NO, KEVIN. YOU BUTT THEM UP AGAINST EACH OTHER, WITHOUT SPACES IN BETWEEN. THEY'RE STUCK TO THE FLOOR WITH A SPECIAL ADHESIVE, AND YOU CAN CUT THEM EASILY WITH A SHARP CRAFT KNIFE. SHALL I GET YOU SOME?'

LET'S SEE. MUM WANTS VINYL TILES IN THE KITCHEN. BLUE ONES, SHE SAID.'

THERE ARE ALL KINDS OF COLOURS AND PATTERNS. VINYL TILES ARE EASY TO CLEAN, WATERPROOF AND VERY HARD-WEARING, SO I'D SAY THEY'RE IDEAL FOR A KITCHEN... ESPECIALLY IF YOU HAVE CHILDREN WHO ARE PRONE TO SPILLING THEIR FOOD AND DRINKS.

I'LL TAKE THESE. CAN YOU GIVE ME THE RIGHT ADHESIVE TO STICK THEM DOWN?

THEY'RE SELF-ADHESIVE. SIMPLY PEEL OFF THE BACKING PAPER AND PRESS THEM DOWN. DO IT CAREFULLY, BECAUSE THEY'RE HARD TO GET OFF AGAIN. AND DO MENTION TO YOUR MOTHER THAT SHE'S WELCOME TO CHANGE THESE IF SHE WANTS A DIFFERENT SHADE – OR PATTERN.

CAPTAIN'S TIP
Self-adhesive tiles will only stick to perfect floors. You may need to lay a sheet of hardboard over a wooden floor, or get a builder to lay a fine surface screed on concrete to make your floor perfectly level.

FOR MORE FLOORING OPTIONS, SEE PAGES 196–205.

CAPTAIN COMPETENT'S

THE FLATPACK FIEND

You can't furnish a home in the 21st century without knowing how to construct a flatpack (unless you have your very own superhero on call). But don't worry — it's hardly rocket science. Just work slowly and methodically, follow the instructions to the letter and apply a bit of common sense. I guess that rules Kevin out, then...

ALL THESE FLATPACK INSTRUCTIONS ARE MAKING MY HEAD SPIN!

WHATEVER YOU WANT TO DO, THERE WILL BE A FLATPACK THAT FITS THE BILL (WELL, MORE OR LESS). READ ON FOR MY SENSATIONAL SECRETS OF FLATPACK SUCCESS.

PLAN THE ROUTES YOU'LL USE MOST OFTEN IN A NEW KITCHEN: FILL KETTLE, MAKE TEA, SIT DOWN WITH FEET UP.

Flatpacks are fabulous! They fit easily into the average car, so no waiting around for unpredictable delivery vans; they're economical; and you can mix and match units to design your own individual creation. BUT flatpacks can also be infuriating – if you're half-way through the construction and find a vital screw missing, or the dowel just won't fit into the predrilled hole, or the instructions are so confusing they might as well be in Swahili! Here are the golden rules of flatpack construction; follow these and you shouldn't go far wrong.

1. MEASURE AND PLAN

Whether you're completely replacing your kitchen units, or just making a simple cabinet, measure every aspect of the space accurately – and remember to leave room for doors to open and essential plumbing to fit. For a big job, make a floor plan and a wall plan so you can check the fit in different dimensions. If you're attaching units to a partition, mark the positions of the studs on your plan, as it will be easier to fix into them. Check walls with a pipe and cable detector, and mark any pipes or cables on the plan, so you know not to drill there. You could use nice colours on your picture, like blue for pipes, red for cables, yellow for light fittings – it'll be a work of art.

2. WHERE ARE YOUR ELECTRIC SOCKETS?

You should never box in sockets behind units, as they could be extremely dangerous in the event of a flood. Consider where you'll need sockets, show an electrician the plan for your new units, and ask him to move any sockets to a suitable position, or install new ones, if necessary.

3. ADDITIONAL EXTRAS

When you've selected your basic flatpack unit, find out if any parts need to be purchased separately. Does your kit include doors, shelves, drawers and cupboard handles? Would you rather fix decorative legs and handles? Make sure any extras are compatible with the base unit.

4. CHECK YOUR BITS AND PIECES

Your kit should consist of the requisite number of pieces of MDF or coated chipboard with predrilled fixing holes; a bag full of fixings; and the all-important instruction sheet. Lay out the large pieces on the floor, arranging them roughly as they will be joined. Do they look as though they are going to make the final product you imagine? Now, sort all the pieces of dowel and screws on a tray, and check they are all there. If anything's missing, go back to the shop and get a replacement pack.

5. WILL THE UNITS REST ON THE FLOOR?

Check that it's level. If there's a slope of more than 12 mm (½ in) along the stretch the units will rest on, your unit doors won't hang properly, and shelves and drawers will be askew. Call in a builder to level the floor. If there's a very slight slope, you should be able to correct it with thin wedges of wood under the sides of each unit.

6. ATTACHING TO WALLS

Check the height of your walls at one end of the unit position and then the other. If they're higher at one end, you know not to take your measurements from ceiling height down – and you're going to have to live with an uneven gap above them. Make sure you know what kind of walls you're drilling into – use the Captain's special tapping and listening technique (see page 58). If you can't arrange your units so that the fixings go into the studs on partition walls, you'll need to buy special, heavy-duty hollow-wall fixings.

7. PAINTS AND FINISHES

If you're planning to apply paint or a finish to the doors or any other part of a unit, it will be easiest if you do it before you attach them – and allow them to dry thoroughly.

8. HAVE YOU GOT ALL THE TOOLS YOU'LL NEED?

One of the most useful tools for bashing flatpack pieces together is a rubber mallet – it's strong enough to be effective, but won't damage the surface. You'll also need screwdrivers (and you'll be grateful for an electric one if you're doing a lot of fixing); a drill and appropriate bits (both twist and countersink, of different sizes); and some wood glue (which may or may not be included in your kit).

9. UNINTERRUPTED SPACE

Make sure you have enough room to work, and that there won't be any children or animals traipsing through and accidentally kicking that crucial fixing nut under the sofa.

10. A MODICUM OF COMMON SENSE

You won't need much of this – flatpacks are easy, if you follow the assembly sequence recommended on the instructions. Always keep an image of the end product in your mind's eye and make sure you seem to be working towards it. If two bits really don't want to fit together, double-check that you haven't made a mistake somewhere down the line. And if you have any parts left over at the end, be afraid. Be very afraid.

REJUVENATING THE KITCHEN...

WITH ONLY A LITTLE HELP FROM A COMPETENT FRIEND

HEY! I THINK I CAN REMEMBER HOW TO DO THIS!

1 One of Kevin's kitchen cupboards has fallen off and it inspires him to give the whole kitchen a makeover. Only problem is that he can't get Caroline to leave, so he has to do everything himself. First of all, he removes the old cupboard doors, supporting them until both hinges have been removed so they don't splinter the wood of the base unit.

2 Kevin fills the crumbled fixing holes where the unit used to hang, and remembers to use his pipe and cable detector before deciding on the new bracket fixing positions. He measures up, marks the spots in pencil and checks they are level. His brow is furrowed in concentration.

I HOPE THIS PIPE AND CABLE DETECTIVE ISN'T DEFECTIVE. THAT WOULD BE RATHER SHOCKING.

3 Kevin drills pilot holes for the fixing brackets, then screws them to the back of his fallen cupboard – checking they're the right way up, of course.

BETTER MAKE SURE I DON'T SCREW UP THIS TIME.

4 Kevin racks his brain and remembers how the Captain fixed a heavy shelf to a masonry wall with long screws and wallplugs. He marks a depth stop on his drill bit with a piece of masking tape, takes a deep breath and switches on the drill with hammer action.

WOW, I'M IMPRESSED. I'M ALWAYS NERVOUS ABOUT DRILLING INTO WALLS.

THERE'S NOTHING TO IT. AHEM.

5 He inserts the plugs, then screws the fixing brackets to the walls.

DID I MEASURE CORRECTLY? WHAT IF THE CUPBOARD BRACKETS ARE IN DIFFERENT PLACES AND DON'T ALIGN WITH THESE ONES? I'LL LOOK VERY SILLY.

IT FITS! THAT'S A MIRACLE! ERM, NO, OF COURSE IT'S NOT. IT'S A RESULT OF CAREFUL PLANNING AND METICULOUS EXECUTION. AHEM. FROG IN MY THROAT.

OH, YOU'RE SUCH A STAR!

6 When Caroline goes out to the shops, Kevin quickly puts on the toolbelt to get some advice from his much more competent friend.

HMM, NOT BAD AT ALL. THE BOY'S DEFINITELY IMPROVING. IF I WAS BEING PICKY – WHICH I AM – I'D HAVE TO POINT OUT THAT THE UNIT'S A TAD OFF HORIZONTAL, BUT I CAN ADJUST THE SCREWS IN THE FIXING BRACKETS TO MAKE IT PERFECTLY LEVEL.

I WONDER HOW LONG CAROLINE WILL BE AWAY? THERE'S A JOB TO BE DONE THAT POOR KEVIN WOULD NEVER MANAGE ON HIS OWN.

7 Kevin wants a new worktop installed, so the Captain is going to do it as fast as he can before Caroline returns. If you are fitting a worktop around a sink, you may wish to call a plumber to drain the pipes and disconnect it for you. Alternatively, scrape out the sealant around all edges of the worktop and unscrew the fixing screws, which you'll find in the cupboards or drawers underneath.

WHOEVER THOUGHT I'D 'SINK' TO THIS LEVEL? HA, HA.

8 Use the sink as a template and draw its outline on to the piece of laminate worktop that you plan to fit around it. Now measure the width of the lip of the sink that will rest on the worktop and draw another line that distance inside the first one.

CAPTAIN'S TIP

Replacing worktops is not a job for the fainthearted! It's only a DIY job if the existing worktops have plain butt corner joints or are in straight runs; otherwise you need special cutting jigs.

9 Drill through the four corners of the inner line you have marked, then use a power jigsaw to cut out the shape the sink will fit in. Don't forget to put on goggles and a dust mask when cutting laminate boards.

DON'T CUT ALONG THE OUTER LINE, OR YOUR SINK WILL JUST FALL THROUGH THE WORKTOP.

10 Measure and cut the rest of the worktop to the lengths required.

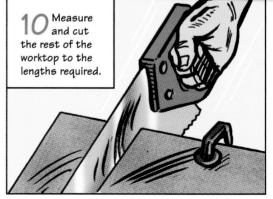

11 The worktop will be screwed down, back and front, every 240 mm (10 in) or so, and at every corner or junction. If you removed the last surface very carefully, it might be possible to reuse the old fixing holes. The Captain is adding some extra screws, so he needs to drill clearance holes through the support rails in the cupboards.

12 Place the worktop in position and refit the sink (or get a plumber to do it).

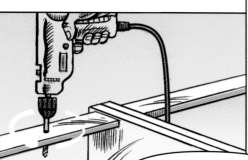

13 Use masking tape to make a depth stop on your drill bit so that you can drill through the clearance holes in the cupboard frame and into the worktop, but without breaking through the surface above (this wouldn't be attractive). Insert wood screws into each of the holes to hold your worktop firmly in place.

LYING IN KEVIN'S SMELLY CUPBOARDS WITH SAWDUST FALLING ON MY FACE IS NOT MY MOST FAVOURITE OCCUPATION. THE THINGS I DO FOR THAT BOY!

14 It's best to plan so that the factory-cut ends of board are on show, because they have neat finishes. If you have any rough edges, you can stick on a strip of laminate trim to tidy them up. Use contact adhesive, press it on firmly and, when it dries, file down any rough edges.

LAMINATE ADHESIVE BONDS INSTANTANEOUSLY. LINE UP YOUR TRIM CAREFULLY BECAUSE YOU WON'T BE ABLE TO MAKE ANY ADJUSTMENTS TO IT LATER.

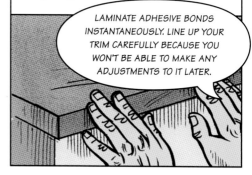

15 Seal all the joints with flexible silicone sealant – along the back where the worktop meets the tiles, around the edges of the sink and between adjoining bits of board – or buy special trim strips for a more professional finish. As he is doing this, the Captain hears Caroline coming back. He slips off the toolbelt... and she finds Kev brandishing the tube of sealant.

THIS LOOKS AMAZING! YOU ARE A SENSATIONAL DIY BOYFRIEND, AND I'M SO SORRY I EVER DOUBTED YOU.

16 Kevin and Caroline are replacing all the cupboard door and drawer fronts, but first they need to fix the handles. She marks the fixing positions with a pencil, then he drills the clearance holes, inserts the screws from behind and screws them into the handles.

17 Cupboard door kits are supplied with the correct screws and hinges, and there will probably be a pre-cut hole where the circular part of the hinge sits in the door. This time, Caroline uses a bradawl to mark the fixing positions, and Kevin screws the hinges into place.

18 Measure and mark the hinge positions in your cupboards. If you're not able to use the same fixing holes as the last hinges, fill the old holes with wood filler and sand them down later. Drill new fixing holes and screw the door hinges into the cabinet.

19 Fortunately, Kevin remembers the way the Captain adjusted the screws on his door hinges so that the door hung level, and opened and closed easily. Look back at page 65 if you've forgotten already (tut, tut).

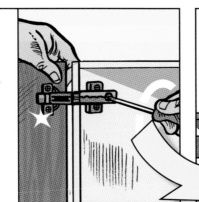

20 Kevin's kitchen drawer fronts are held in place with glued dowels, so he bought replacements that are fitted in the same way (*see page 65 to remind yourself how it's done*). There are different options with other kinds of drawer unit, though...

Flatpack drawers sometimes have a retaining clip that is screwed on to the drawer front, then inserted into a matching clip sunk into the drawer side. The fixing holes will normally be pre-drilled, and the only thing you have to take care about is to get the drawer front the right way up – they'll be marked 'top' and 'bottom', so it's not <u>too</u> challenging.

ALTERNATIVELY

Some drawers have false fronts, attached to the basic box shape with countersunk screws inserted from the inside, but not so far that they pierce the outside. These are easy to replace – simply unscrew the existing front and attach the replacement. Make sure it is centred across the drawer width – and that it's not so wide that it will prevent you from opening the drawers on either side!

YOU'VE DONE A WONDERFUL JOB IN HERE. I'M SO PROUD OF YOU.

DON'T FORGET I HAD A LITTLE HELP. AHEM. FROM YOU, I MEAN.

KEVIN'S INCREDIBLE STORAGE UNIT

MAYBE I SHOULD TAKE MY NEW-FOUND CUPBOARD KNOWLEDGE AND USE IT TO TIDY UP MY MOVIE AND MUSIC COLLECTIONS BEFORE THEY TAKE OVER THE SITTING ROOM COMPLETELY. LET ME SEE...

I WONDER IF THIS WOULD WORK? IT WOULD CERTAINLY HELP TO ORGANISE MY CLUTTER.

He measures everything – even the dimensions of his videos, CDs and DVDs.

IF A VIDEO IS 190 MM TALL, 25 MM WIDE AND 100 MM DEEP, HOW MANY COULD I GET IN A BASIC UNIT OF, SAY 750 X 750 MM? YIKES! I NEED A MATHEMATICIAN HERE.

THE ANSWER TO YOUR QUESTION IS 90 (30 PER SHELF), ALLOWING SPACE FOR THE WIDTH OF TWO SHELVES. YOU COULD HAVE SEVERAL MORE ROWS BEHIND IF YOU DIDN'T MIND NOT BEING ABLE TO READ THE TITLES AT A GLANCE. BUT WE HAVE BASIC UNITS OF MANY DIFFERENT SIZES. LET'S SEE...

MAYBE I'LL JUST TAKE FIVE BASIC UNITS OF A STANDARD SIZE AND PLAY AROUND WITH THE SHELF POSITIONS AT HOME.

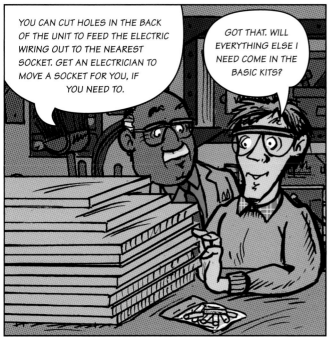

YOU CAN CUT HOLES IN THE BACK OF THE UNIT TO FEED THE ELECTRIC WIRING OUT TO THE NEAREST SOCKET. GET AN ELECTRICIAN TO MOVE A SOCKET FOR YOU, IF YOU NEED TO.

GOT THAT. WILL EVERYTHING ELSE I NEED COME IN THE BASIC KITS?

THE SHELVES, DOORS AND DOOR HANDLES COME SEPARATELY. I'LL GIVE YOU 12 SHELVES FOR NOW, BUT COME BACK IF YOU NEED ANY MORE. AND DON'T WORRY. JUST FOLLOW THE INSTRUCTIONS AND YOU WON'T GO FAR WRONG. WELL, YOU SHOULDN'T...

I'M NOT SURE I CAN MANAGE THIS ON MY OWN. WHAT ON EARTH IS A LOCKING CAM? I DON'T WANT TO RUIN CAROLINE'S OPINION OF ME, SO I'D BETTER PREVAIL ON THE CAPTAIN AGAIN.

What a wimp you are, Kevin! A locking cam is a simple way of attaching two pieces at an angle of 90°, and there are full instructions on the sheet you're holding in front of you.

WISE MOVE, KEVIN. THEY DON'T CALL ME THE FLATPACK FIEND FOR NOTHING. I'LL WHIP THIS UNIT TOGETHER IN NO TIME AT ALL.

1 The Captain screws the legs to the underside of the first base panel, then turns it right side up.

TWO LEGS GOOD, FOUR LEGS BETTER. ANYONE READ 'ANIMAL FARM'?

2 Screw the fixing studs to the four corners, following the instruction sheet, then apply PVA wood glue to some dowels and insert them into the pre-drilled holes along the sides of your base panel. Tap them gently with a rubber mallet if it's tricky to get them in.

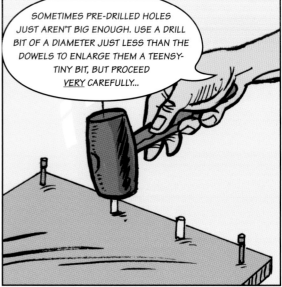

SOMETIMES PRE-DRILLED HOLES JUST AREN'T BIG ENOUGH. USE A DRILL BIT OF A DIAMETER JUST LESS THAN THE DOWELS TO ENLARGE THEM A TEENSY-TINY BIT, BUT PROCEED _VERY_ CAREFULLY...

3 Insert the locking cams into the side panels, in the places marked. Apply a dab of glue to the tops of the dowels you've inserted along the sides of the base panel, and you're ready to put the first side in position.

4 Hold your side panel at right angles above the base panel and align the grooves where the back panel will slide in. Push the side panel into place carefully, letting the dowels slip into the pre-drilled holes and the fixing studs into the locking cams.

GO GENTLY WITH THE DOWELS – THEY'RE FLIMSY CRITTERS. I'VE BROKEN DOZENS OF THEM OVER THE CENTURIES. BUT IT WAS NEVER MY FAULT, OF COURSE.

5 Tighten the locking cams, making sure the arrows point in the right direction. Your first side panel should be standing upright all by itself.

6 Apply a little glue into the groove along the back of the base panel and up the side of the side panel where the back will slide into place. Then fit the back into place. Carefully.

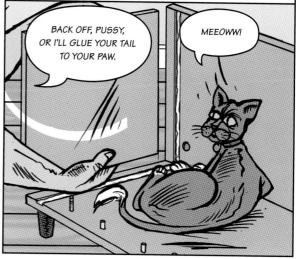

7 Glue the tops of the dowels and the groove on the other side panel, then position it just as you did for the first, except you have to make sure that the back panel slots into the groove as well as fitting the dowels into their holes. Tighten the locking cams. (And watch out for vengeful cats.)

8 Insert the four fixing studs in the corners of the top panel of the unit. Glue and stick in the dowels, and glue the groove along the back of the top panel. Place the top of your cabinet in position so the back panel fits in the groove and the dowels sit in their holes. Tap it gently with the rubber mallet till it all sits flush, then tighten the locking cams.

WHERE'S KEVIN'S PLAN GONE? I CAN'T REMEMBER WHERE HE SAID HE WANTED SHELVES TO GO. OH WELL, I'LL JUST JUDGE FOR MYSELF. I'LL PROBABLY ARRANGE THEM MUCH BETTER THAN HE DID.

9 Mark the positions where you want your shelves. There are several different ways of fixing shelves in flatpack units. Some have metal supports that the shelves slide on to. Others have small wooden blocks for the shelves to sit on. The shelves in Kevin's units snap into place on top of fixing screws that you attach in the cabinet sides.

THE SCREWS SUPPLIED ARE THE RIGHT LENGTH SO THAT THEY WON'T SCREW RIGHT OUT THE OTHER SIDE OF THE UNIT. DON'T SWITCH THEM FOR OTHER ONES, WHICH MIGHT!

10 The Captain inserts two fixing screws into each side of the cabinet and checks they are level with each other. Then he knocks the inserts that will fit over the screws into the shelves.

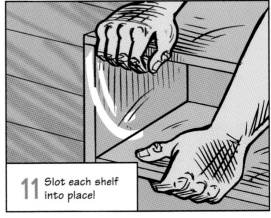

11 Slot each shelf into place!

12 Before you can even say 'Stupendous, Scintillating Superhero', the Captain has knocked up the other four base units and is fixing shelves in them — at random, it seems.

WHAT WAS IT AGAIN? THIS ONE FOR VIDEOS AND MAGAZINES, THIS ONE FOR CDS AND – WHAT ELSE? KITTY, YOU SIT IN THERE MUCH LONGER AND I'LL HANG THE DOOR ON AND NAIL IT CLOSED.

13 Each flatpack cabinet panel will have four joining points marked on their inside corners. It's simple to join units at those points. Mark your drill bit with a depth stop so that you go through the first unit and just into, but not through, the next. Insert the screws and screw the units together. The Captain ignores the joining points and plans his own design.

IF ONLY KEVIN HAD BOUGHT SIX UNITS, I COULD HAVE PUT THE LAST ONE ON TOP AND MADE A PYRAMID SHAPE.

14 The Captain is marking where he's going to cut holes for the electric flexes to trail out to the socket.

15 He uses a drill with a flat bit to make holes for the flexes. Insert plastic protectors called grommets if you're doing this at home, to make sure the flexes don't rub against rough wood, which could cause their sheathing to chafe and wear.

LET THE MUSIC PLAY!

16 Working almost at the speed of light (but not quite), the Captain attaches the door handles and then the doors. If you've forgotten how to do this, check back on page 178 for the method.

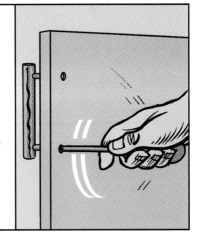

HMM, THAT'S NOT EXACTLY THE ARRANGEMENT I HAD IN MIND, BUT I MUST SAY THE CAPTAIN HAS WORKED QUICKLY.

OH-OH. THIS ISN'T VERY HANDY. MAYBE MY CAPTAIN ISN'T QUITE SO COMPETENT AFTER ALL!

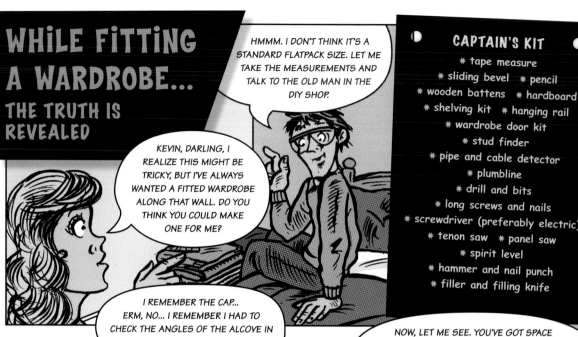

HMMM. I DON'T THINK IT'S A STANDARD FLATPACK SIZE. LET ME TAKE THE MEASUREMENTS AND TALK TO THE OLD MAN IN THE DIY SHOP.

CAPTAIN'S KIT
* tape measure
* sliding bevel * pencil
* wooden battens * hardboard
* shelving kit * hanging rail
* wardrobe door kit
* stud finder
* pipe and cable detector
* plumbline
* drill and bits
* long screws and nails
* screwdriver (preferably electric)
* tenon saw * panel saw
* spirit level
* hammer and nail punch
* filler and filling knife

KEVIN, DARLING, I REALIZE THIS MIGHT BE TRICKY, BUT I'VE ALWAYS WANTED A FITTED WARDROBE ALONG THAT WALL. DO YOU THINK YOU COULD MAKE ONE FOR ME?

I REMEMBER THE CAP... ERM, NO... I REMEMBER I HAD TO CHECK THE ANGLES OF THE ALCOVE IN MY SITTING ROOM WITH A SLIDING BEVEL WHEN I WAS FITTING SHELVES THERE.

1 Kevin measures the height, depth and width of the area at different points, and uses a sliding bevel to check the angles where the walls meet (*see page 131 to refresh your memory*). He makes a scale drawing with the measurements marked on it, using all his hidden artistic talent.

NOW, LET ME SEE. YOU'VE GOT SPACE ACROSS THE FRONT HERE TO ACCOMMODATE TWO READY-MADE FLATPACK WARDROBE DOORS – THAT WILL BE MUCH EASIER THAN MAKING YOUR OWN. YOU'LL JUST HAVE TO CONSTRUCT A BASIC FRAMEWORK AND COVER IT IN MDF. HAVE YOU EVER DONE THAT?

GULP. NO...NEVER.

HERE'S HOW I WOULD DO IT. YOUR HANGING SPACE NEEDS A DEPTH OF AT LEAST 510 MM (20 IN) TO ACCOMMODATE THE WIDTH OF A COATHANGER – BUT THERE'S PLENTY OF ROOM, SO THAT'S FINE.

I'M STILL NOT VERY CLEAR ABOUT HOW I MAKE THE ACTUAL FRAME.

CUT THESE SOFTWOOD BATTENS TO SIZE AND NAIL THEM TO THE CEILING, FLOOR AND WALLS TO MAKE THE SHAPE I'VE DRAWN FOR YOU, THEN ATTACH YOUR MDF SHEETS ON TOP. FIT THE DOORS AND THE HANGING RAIL – AND YOU CAN PUT SHELVING ON ONE SIDE, IF YOU LIKE.

AH, I KNOW HOW TO DO SHELVING.

THAT LOOKS TERRIFIC, KEVIN. I'VE GOT A HAIRDRESSER'S APPOINTMENT NOW, BUT MAYBE WE COULD START ON IT LATER?

I'LL, ERM, CONSTRUCT THE FRAME WHILE YOU'RE OUT, THEN WE CAN WORK TOGETHER PUTTING IN THE SHELVES AND HANGING THE DOORS. OK?

PHEW! THAT WAS A CLOSE SHAVE! HOW COULD I TELL HER THAT I COULD NO MORE BUILD THIS FRAME MYSELF THAN DESIGN A SPACE STATION? I HAVEN'T A CLUE WHERE TO START. BETTER PUT THE TOOLBELT ON.

2 Find the way the ceiling joists run by using a stud finder, or go into your attic and poke a bradawl through the ceiling along a joist; alternatively, do some test drillings. The wardrobe's ceiling plates should be attached to joists, while the floor plates will be screwed into the floor. Plan your fixing positions, avoiding any pipes and cables, of course. You may have to alter your plans if the joists aren't where you want them (and they hardly ever are).

I DON'T KNOW WHY I SHOULD HELP THAT BOY ANY MORE AFTER HE CRITICISED MY FABULOUS STORAGE CABINETS. STILL, WE SUPERHEROES HAVE A SOCIAL RESPONSIBILITY... BESIDES, IT'S ALL FOR THE LOVELY CAROLINE.

3 There are two ceiling plates – one along the back of the alcove and the other at the front of the unit. Two floor plates should be attached directly underneath them. Use a plumbline to mark their fixing positions on the bedroom floor.

PULL FLOOR COVERINGS OUT OF THE WAY SO YOU CAN ATTACH FLOOR PLATES DIRECTLY ON TO THE FLOOR. FLUFFY CARPETS PLAY HAVOC WITH YOUR MEASUREMENTS.

4 Cut the ceiling plates to length with a panel saw. Hold them up to mark the fixing holes so that screws will penetrate the joists. Drill clearance holes through the ceiling plates and attach them to the ceiling with countersunk wood screws.

MERE MORTALS WILL NEED A HELPER TO HOLD THE PLATES IN POSITION AS THEY SCREW THEM IN. NEEDLESS TO SAY, THIS IS NOT A PROBLEM FOR ME.

5 Cut and attach your floor plates in the same way as you attached the ceiling plates in step 4. Use your plumbline again to check they're exactly beneath the ceiling plates – or you'll run into trouble later on (very soon, in fact).

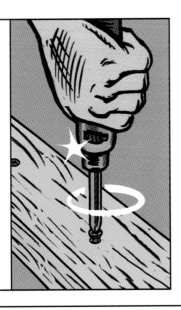

6 Measure and cut your vertical battens. This frame has six – one at each corner and two in the centre, back and front. Mark vertical guidelines for the four that will be attached to the side walls (at the back and the front). Measure and cut your battens so that they fit tightly between the floor and ceiling plates.

7 Position the vertical battens. If the skirting is in the way, you will have to cut notches so that they fit neatly around it. Mark the shape in pencil, then cut the notches with a tenon saw.

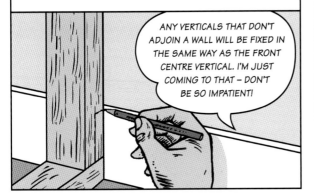

ANY VERTICALS THAT DON'T ADJOIN A WALL WILL BE FIXED IN THE SAME WAY AS THE FRONT CENTRE VERTICAL. I'M JUST COMING TO THAT – DON'T BE SO IMPATIENT!

8 Mark fixing holes on the vertical battens that will be fixed to the walls. Make the first one just above the skirting, then space the rest roughly 450 mm (18 in) apart. Drill clearance holes and screw the battens on to the walls.

WANNA LEARN ABOUT SKEWING? READ ON...

9 To fix each centre batten in place, position it between the floor and ceiling plates, and use a wooden block to support it at right angles while you 'skew' in nails to fix it. Use 100 mm (4 in) nails and hammer them at an angle down through the vertical and into the horizontal plate. Use a nail punch to get the nail heads flush with the surface of the wood. Repeat on the opposite side of the vertical, then do the same at the top, skewing nails through the vertical into the ceiling plate.

THAT'S THEM WELL AND TRULY SKEWED.

10 Measure and cut three battens for each side of your frame. One will run between the two ceiling plates, one between the two floor plates and the third will be at the level where you want a shelf to run above the hanging space. (Before you decide on the shelf position, hold a few of your longer garments in the hanging space to see how much room they need.) Attach the battens to the side walls.

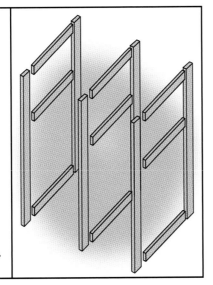

11 The basic framework is now ready to be covered. Measure the sides and back, then the top and bottom of the frame, and mark your cutting positions on the MDF. Don't forget to include a divider to go down the middle of the wardrobe, separating the hanging part from the shelving space. Leave the front for now.

BEFORE STICKING UP THE MDF LINING, CHECK YOUR FRAMEWORK WITH A SPIRIT LEVEL TO MAKE SURE THE HAMMERING AND SCREWING HASN'T KNOCKED ANYTHING OUT OF TRUE. MINE IS FINE – I'M A PRETTY STRAIGHT KIND OF A GUY.

12 Remember to wear a dust mask when you cut MDF, to avoid inhaling particles.

PARTITION WALLS THAT DIVIDE ROOMS IN TWO ARE MADE IN THE SAME WAY AS THIS FRAMEWORK. JUST ADD MORE VERTICAL AND HORIZONTAL BATTENS SO THAT THERE'S ONE EVERY 500 MM (20 IN) OR SO IN EITHER DIRECTION.

13 Fix the MDF around your frame using nails spaced at roughly 150 mm (6 in) intervals along each batten. Butt the pieces tightly up to each other. Mark the position of the horizontal battens at shelf level on the inside of your lining.

FOR A PARTITION WALL, YOU WOULD COVER BOTH SIDES OF THE FRAME IN PLASTERBOARD.

IF YOU WANT TO TIDY UP THE APPEARANCE OF THE INSIDE OF YOUR WARDROBE, YOU CAN SPREAD FILLER OVER THE JOINTS, COVERING THE NAIL HEADS. TAPER IT OUTWARDS, THEN SAND IT AND PAINT IT LATER.

14 Attach some small battens through the lining and into the horizontal shelf supports, then cut out the upper shelf. Rest it on the battens and insert a few fixing screws up through the battens and just into the shelf above (*see page 131 if you need a reminder of how to do this*).

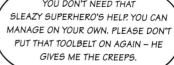

15 Working in harmony, they put up the shelves Caroline wants, using the same kind of shelf fixings as Kevin has in his storage cabinet (*see page 184 if you've forgotten already*).

16 Last but not least, no wardrobe is complete without a hanging rail. The Old Man had sold Kevin a sturdy metal rail with fixing brackets that screw into the sides of the wardrobe. Caroline wisely puts a coathanger on it so they can judge the correct depth, then Kevin secures the fixings all on his own, remembering to fit the rail before attaching the second bracket.

17 Kevin puts the hinges on his wardrobe doors, then attaches them to the wardrobe frame. (*See page 178 for a reminder of how to fit flatpack doors.*)

I KNOW. AND YOU WERE ENJOYING TAKING THE CREDIT FOR HIS WORK. YOU DON'T NEED HIM ANY MORE, THOUGH. YOU'RE MUCH MORE COMPETENT THAN YOU THINK YOU ARE.

I'M SO SORRY I DIDN'T TELL YOU ABOUT THE CAPTAIN BEFORE. IT JUST SEEMED SO WEIRD.

On his way home, Kevin stops in to visit his nieces. They still haven't dared to use the wonky bunk beds he made them. With his brand-new flatpack knowledge, Kevin can see where he went wrong (more or less everywhere). There should never be any parts left over at the end of a flatpack construction, and all the pre-drilled holes should have some kind of fixing in them. This may explain why none of his horizontals or verticals is true.

SORRY ABOUT THE BEDS, GIRLS, BUT I'M HERE TO PUT THEM RIGHT NOW.

Kevin realizes that he has no choice but to take the beds apart, refix and straighten the basic frame, then build it again – preferably following the instruction sheet this time.

WHY DON'T YOU TRY IT OUT? IT'S SAFE, NOW – I PROMISE.

YOU TRY IT FIRST. IF THE TOP BUNK CAN TAKE YOUR WEIGHT, WE MIGHT SLEEP IN IT TONIGHT.

ZZZZZZZZ...

Kevin lies on the top bunk and closes his eyes. It's been a long, hard day. He's thinking how sweet it is that Caroline seems to believe in him – maybe she's right that he can do everything himself now. He begins to nod off.

Kevin is dreaming of new DIY projects... a swimming pool, a four-poster bed, a fireman's pole from his bedroom to the kitchen for picking up late-night snacks...

DREAM ON, KEVIN. THERE ARE SEVERAL MORE PRACTICAL PROJECTS TO CHALLENGE YOU IN THE NEXT SECTION.

CAPTAIN COMPETENT'S

A SUPERHERO FINISH

If you've sailed through all the other tasks the Captain has explained to you, then you shouldn't have trouble with the finishing touches described here. However, if you're still hitting your thumb instead of the nail, splintering wood with your saw and creating huge holes in the wall every time you pick up a power drill, then do us all a favour. Accept your limitations, hang up your toolbelt and leave these jobs to a professional.

KEVIN GETS CARPETED
BEDROOM TALK

YEEUCH! A PINK CARPET IS NOT THE RIGHT STYLE FOR A MAN-ABOUT-TOWN'S BEDROOM. IT'S TIME FOR A CHANGE IN HERE.

CAPTAIN'S KIT

* paper underlay
* staples and staple gun
* foam-backed carpet
* craft knife and rule
* double-sided tape and carpet adhesive
* threshold strip
* hammer and nails
* bolster chisel
* tack lifter
* stair pads and angled gripper strips
* nail punch
* strip of wood
* wooden spatula
* carpet tacks

1 Kevin's freshly papered bedroom still doesn't look quite right. It takes him a while to put his finger on the problem — or his toes, more like.

2 He carefully measures and jots down the floor area in the bedroom. If you have alcoves in yours, remember to include them in the total length and width of your area. Make a floor plan to show to your carpet dealer.

3 To work out how much carpet is needed for stairs, measure a tread and multiply this by the total number of treads; then measure a riser and multiply by the total number of risers; add your figures together and add an extra length equivalent to the depth of the bottom tread and the height of the bottom riser. Check the width of the carpet needed and measure the area required for the landing at the top. If you have a bend in your stairs, you'll have to measure down where the long edge of the carpet will run to be sure you have enough.

I SHOULD FIX THAT LOOSE CARPET ON MY STAIRS AS WELL TO PREVENT ANY EARLY-MORNING ROLLOVERS...

USE FOAM-BACKED CARPET IN THE BEDROOM; IT'S EASY TO FIT AND ONLY NEEDS A PAPER UNDERLAY. HESSIAN-BACKED CARPETS NEED TO BE STRETCHED INTO PLACE ACROSS A ROOM AND THEY REQUIRE PROPER UNDERLAY, SO IT'S A JOB THAT'S BEST LEFT TO PROFESSIONAL CARPET FITTERS.

SO I JUST TACK IT DOWN AROUND THE EDGES, DO I?

NO TACKING REQUIRED. YOU CAN STICK DOWN THE BEDROOM CARPET WITH DOUBLE-SIDED TAPE AROUND THE EDGES, OR WITH SPRAY-ON CARPET ADHESIVE. FOAM-BACKED CARPET ISN'T SUITABLE FOR STAIRS BECAUSE THEY NEED TO BE EXTRA-SECURE, SO YOU SHOULD USE A HESSIAN-BACKED CARPET HELD IN PLACE WITH GRIPPER STRIPS.

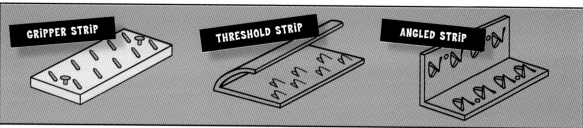

GRIPPER STRIP

THRESHOLD STRIP

ANGLED STRIP

Gripper strips are nailed or stuck to wood or concrete floors, and hessian-backed carpet is pressed down on to them so that it engages with the gripper pins.

Threshold strips have spikes that grip carpet in doorways. They can be single-sided, or double if there's carpet on both sides of the door. Nail or glue them into place.

Angled grippers are nailed on stairs at the junctions between the treads and the risers. There are two rows of spikes to grip the carpet on each side of the strip.

I'VE ALWAYS FANCIED A SHAG-PILE CARPET. NOT SURE EXACTLY WHAT IT IS, BUT THE NAME SOUNDS COOL.

SHAG-PILE IS AT LEAST 25–50 MM (1–2 IN) LONG, AND YOU SHOULDN'T USE IT ON STAIRS. I RECOMMEND YOU OPT FOR A SHORT, DENSE-FIBRE CARPET FOR DURABILITY AND SAFETY'S SAKE. WHAT COLOURS WERE YOU THINKING OF?

CAROLINE THINKS I SHOULD GO FOR A NEUTRAL SAND COLOUR

SHE'S A YOUNG LADY OF IMPECCABLE TASTE (IN CARPETS AT LEAST). GOOD LUCK WITH YOUR LAYING!

4 Remove the old carpet. If it is tacked down, ease out the tacks with a tack lifter. Check the condition of your floorboards and hammer down any loose ones, following the instructions on pages 102–3. Sweep them clean and you're ready to start laying.

5 Unroll the paper underlay and lay it along the first wall, leaving a gap around the edges so that the carpet tape can be stuck directly to the floor. The Old Man has lent Kevin a staple gun so that he can staple his underlay to the floorboards, but you could also use a hammer to tap in large-headed tacks.

LAST TIME I USED A STAPLER, I MANAGED TO STAPLE THE SLEEVE OF MY JUMPER TO A DESK. I WONDER IF IT'S SAFE FOR ME TO DO THIS ON MY OWN? CAROLINE DOESN'T WANT ME TO TRANSFORM MYSELF INTO THE CAPTAIN ANY MORE, BUT I'LL SEE HOW I GO.

6 Kevin finishes stapling the paper underlay without any accidents. When you've finished yours, unroll the carpet and arrange it with the pile running away from the main light source. If you have a patterned carpet, the pattern should run parallel to the main axis of the room. Allow the carpet to overlap the skirting by about 25 mm (1 in).

IT FEELS SMOOTH IN THIS DIRECTION, SO IT SHOULD RUN THIS WAY AROUND, AWAY FROM THE WINDOW. ER, I THINK...

7 To get your carpet to lie flat in alcoves or doorways, use a craft knife to make a diagonal cut in from the edge of the carpet to floor level at each of the corners. Press the carpet flat on the floor with a steel rule. Don't trim it yet if you're planning to stick it down with double-sided tape.

IT SEEMS TO BE GOING OK SO FAR, BUT I'M FEELING VER-RY NERVOUS.

8 Roll back the carpet from the wall again and stick double-sided tape all around the perimeter of the room. If you need two pieces of carpet to cover your floor, stick tape along the join where they meet.

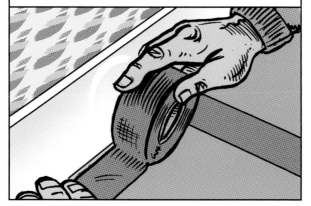

ALTERNATIVELY

If you're using a spray-on carpet adhesive, wait until you've trimmed all the edges to fit before rolling them back and spraying a line of adhesive around the edges of the floor and pressing the carpet down on to it.

9 Remove the backing paper from the double-sided tape, roll the carpet down into position again and press it firmly into the edges using a steel rule. Trim off the edges with a craft knife held at a 45° angle, with the blade facing the skirting; this helps to avoid gaps between the carpet and the skirting.

THAT LOOKS REMARKABLY NEAT. EAT YOUR HEART OUT, CAPTAIN.

10 If you need to fit carpet around radiator pipes, use a craft knife to cut a slit from the edge, cut out a circle for the pipe, then apply adhesive to the cut pieces before you press them down around the pipe. Treat other obstructions in a similar way. In the door opening, press the carpet down with the edge of a bolster chisel and use a craft knife held at a 45° angle to trim carefully around the moulding.

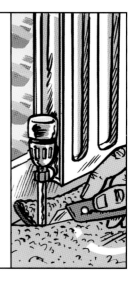

11 If you have two pieces of carpet meeting anywhere, apply a line of carpet adhesive along the edges of one of them. Peel off the backing paper from the double-sided tape and press both edges down onto it. Wipe off any excess adhesive that oozes out of the join.

12 Nail a length of threshold strip across the doorway (checking there are no pipe or cable runs underneath – if there are, then glue it down with some contact adhesive). Use the edge of a bolster chisel to tuck your carpet neatly underneath.

13 Kevin has lifted his stair carpet and is using a tack lifter to remove stray tacks from the stairs. He's getting increasingly anxious, though.

> I'VE GOT MY STAIR PADS AND ANGLED GRIPPERS, BUT I CAN'T QUITE FIGURE OUT HOW TO PUT IT ALL TOGETHER. I'M GOING TO HAVE TO CAVE IN AND ASK FOR HELP. PLEASE, CAPTAIN. PRETTY PLEASE.

14 The Captain positions a stair pad on the top step and nails an angled gripper down through it into the tread, then horizontally into the riser. Use a nail punch to knock the nails right in. The edge of the stair pad overhangs the front of the tread and should be tacked or stapled on to the riser below.

> IF A JOB'S WORTH DOING, IT'S A SHAME TO LEAVE IT TO AMATEURS. LOOSE STAIR CARPET IS LETHAL!

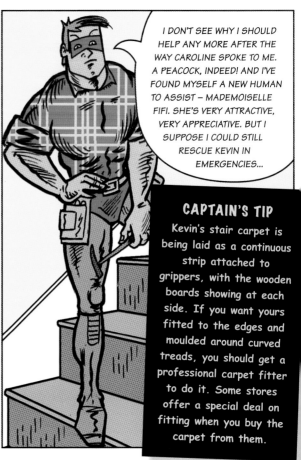

> I DON'T SEE WHY I SHOULD HELP ANY MORE AFTER THE WAY CAROLINE SPOKE TO ME. A PEACOCK, INDEED! AND I'VE FOUND MYSELF A NEW HUMAN TO ASSIST – MADEMOISELLE FIFI. SHE'S VERY ATTRACTIVE, VERY APPRECIATIVE. BUT I SUPPOSE I COULD STILL RESCUE KEVIN IN EMERGENCIES...

CAPTAIN'S TIP
Kevin's stair carpet is being laid as a continuous strip attached to grippers, with the wooden boards showing at each side. If you want yours fitted to the edges and moulded around curved treads, you should get a professional carpet fitter to do it. Some stores offer a special deal on fitting when you buy the carpet from them.

15 Apply pads and grippers all the way down the stairs, but don't fit a pad on the bottom step. Unroll the carpet and position it roughly, making sure the pile will run down the stairs (and that you've got the right length). Now roll it up again, turn it over and place the bottom end upside down on the bottom step, and hammer a gripper in place on top of it at the angle where the tread meets the riser.

> YEP! THERE'S NO PAD ON THE BOTTOM STEP – JUST AN UPSIDE-DOWN LAYER OF CARPET, WHICH WILL BE COVERED UP BY A RIGHT-WAY-UP LAYER.

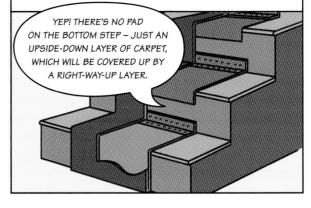

16 Smooth the carpet over the last tread and down the last riser to the hall floor. Nail a strip of wood through the carpet at the point where it meets the hall floor.

YOU DON'T UNDERSTAND WHAT I'M DOING YET, DO YOU? WAIT AND SEE.

17 Bend the carpet up over the strip of wood and smooth it over the first few steps. Use a wooden spatula to get the backing of the carpet to engage on the teeth of the gripper between the first tread and the second riser. Make sure it is hooked on both sides.

IF YOU'VE FOLLOWED THE INSTRUCTIONS CORRECTLY, YOUR BOTTOM STAIR WILL NOW HAVE CARPET THAT IS THE RIGHT SIDE OUT.

18 Work your way up the stairs, forcing the carpet to engage in the teeth of the grippers. When you reach the top of the last riser, fold over about 25 mm (1 in) of carpet and tack the fold down along the riser.

I'M GOING TO LEAVE KEVIN TO CARPET THE TOP LANDING – HE'S NOT DONE THE BEDROOM TOO BADLY. ALTHOUGH, OBVIOUSLY, I WOULD HAVE DONE IT MUCH BETTER.

19 Lay the landing carpet just as you did the bedroom carpet, but stretch it down over the top step and tack it along the top of the last riser. Stick down the landing carpet all the way around with glue or tape.

HOLY COW! I HEAR THE SOUND OF ANOTHER DIY DISASTER IN TOWN. I MUST DASH.

I WONDER IF I SHOULD CONFESS TO CAROLINE THAT THE CAPTAIN DID THE STAIRS? OR LET HER THINK IT WAS ME... MMMM.

SHEET VINYL
GETTING LAID ON THE KITCHEN FLOOR

SOUNDS AS THOUGH YOU NEED SHEET VINYL. THERE'S A GREAT CHOICE OF COLOURS AND PATTERNS. THE CUSHIONED TYPE IS MOST COMFORTABLE TO WALK ON, AND IT CAN BE LOOSE LAID AS WELL.

WHAT'S THE BEST TYPE OF FLOOR COVERING FOR A KITCHEN? IT NEEDS TO BE WATERPROOF, STAINPROOF, EASY TO CLEAN – AND EASY TO FIT AS WELL.

CAPTAIN'S KIT
* spirit level * sheet vinyl
* block of wood and nail * hammer
* strong scissors * steel rule
* craft knife * bolster chisel
* vinyl adhesive * notched spreader
* threshold bar * pipe and cable detector
* hammer and nails

YOUR KITCHEN'S TOO BIG FOR A SINGLE SHEET, BUT YOU CAN HAVE A JOINT DOWN THE MIDDLE, SO LONG AS IT DOESN'T HIT A DOOR FRAME OR AN AREA THAT YOU WALK ON A LOT. YOU'LL NEED ADHESIVE TO STICK DOWN JOINTS, BUT THE REST CAN BE LEFT LOOSE.

HMM, I'LL GO FOR GREEN VINYL LIKE THE ONE IN CAROLINE'S KITCHEN, I'M SURE SHE'LL APPROVE. HERE ARE MY MEASUREMENTS – HOW MUCH DO YOU THINK I'LL NEED?

Kevin hasn't quite finished with flooring yet.

LET IT ACCLIMATIZE IN THE ROOM WHERE IT WILL BE LAID FOR 48 HOURS.

THANKS A LOT, OLD MAN. YOU'RE A STAR! I'LL GO AND START STRAIGHT AWAY.

WHOOPS-A-DAISY! I WONDER IF I SHOULD LAY IT WITH AN OVERLAP THEN TRIM IT AS I DID WITH THE CARPET? MAYBE I'LL JUST CHECK WHAT THE CAPTAIN THINKS...

1 Check that your floor surface is level. If not, get a builder to level concrete with self-levelling compound, or lay sheets of hardboard over boards. Sweep up any loose grit, which could damage the vinyl, and check that any nail heads are punched well below the surface. If possible, it's best to acclimatize the vinyl unrolled on the floor – but loosely rolled up is almost as good.

2 Arrange your vinyl so that any pattern is squared in the room, and any joints run away from the main light source. Kevin butts his vinyl up to the longest wall – and realizes it doesn't fit, because the wall isn't exactly straight.

3 The Captain makes a 'scriber' – a block of wood with a nail driven through it 50 mm (2 in) from the end, so that the nail tip just protrudes on the other side. He positions the vinyl about 38 mm (1½ in) from the wall, then runs the scriber along it with one edge butting against the wall so that the protruding nail marks a cutting line on the vinyl.

I LEARNED THIS NEAT LITTLE TRICK FROM MY SUPERHERO PAPA. KEVIN WILL HAVE TO MANAGE THE REST OF THE JOB HIMSELF, THOUGH, BECAUSE MADEMOISELLE FIFI NEEDS ME TODAY.

4 Kevin trims along the cutting line on the first sheet of vinyl, and it butts neatly up to the wall. He arranges the second piece, overlapping the first so that the pattern matches. Then he scribes to fit the longest edge of the second piece along the opposite wall, just as the Captain had done.

IT'S WEIRD, BUT ONCE THE CAPTAIN HAS DONE SOMETHING, I ALWAYS REMEMBER HOW TO DO IT MYSELF NEXT TIME. HE'S A GOOD TEACHER.

5 Trim the other edges to fit by pressing a steel rule against them and trimming along it with a craft knife. When you reach an internal corner, cut a triangular piece off the vinyl so you can press it flat on each side. At an external corner, cut a diagonal line through the excess up to the corner and press it flat.

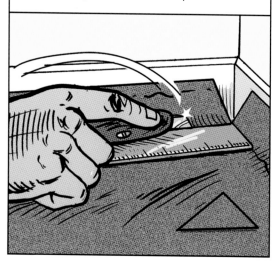

6 Use a bolster chisel to press the vinyl into the angle between the skirting and the floor (or the floor and the kitchen units).

I SUPPOSE THE CAPTAIN'S A BOLSTER FOR MY CONFIDENCE. HA, HA... OH, YIKES! I SEEM TO BE PICKING UP HIS PROPENSITY FOR PUNS!

7 Where the two sheets of vinyl overlap, use a steel rule and a craft knife to cut a straight line through both layers.

> IT'S NOT JUST THE CAPTAIN. I CAN BE CUTTING TOO.

8 Remove the waste strips, then fold back the two edges and apply vinyl adhesive to the floor with a notched spreader (or use double-sided tape). Press the edges down firmly.

CAPTAIN'S TIP
The adhesive used to stick down sheet vinyl is extremely flammable, so make sure all naked flames are extinguished and that the room is well ventilated.

9 When you reach a door frame, press the vinyl down into the angle between the frame and the floor, and use a craft knife to cut it to the exact shape. An easier alternative is to slip the vinyl under the architrave, as you did for wood-strip flooring (see page 116).

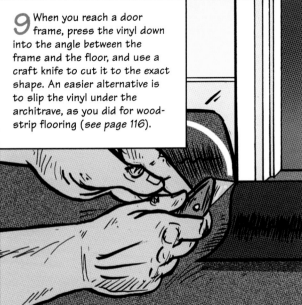

> I THINK I'LL FIT ONE OF THOSE NICE THRESHOLD BARS HERE. I'LL JUST NEED A ONE-SIDED BAR, BECAUSE THERE IS A WOODEN FLOOR ON THE OTHER SIDE.

10 Don't forget to check the floor with a pipe and cable detector before you nail down a threshold bar. If you find pipes or cables there, just glue it down with instant-grip adhesive. Tuck the vinyl neatly under it with a bolster chisel. Lean back and admire.

I LIKE A NICE FINISH. CAROLINE'S GOING TO BE VERY PROUD OF ME. I WONDER IF THAT'S HER NOW ON THE PHONE?

I'M AT AN AUCTION ROOM, AND THEY HAVE SOME WONDERFUL OLD FURNITURE AND A FANTASTIC FIREPLACE SURROUND. IF I BUY THEM, DO YOU THINK WE COULD RENOVATE THEM BETWEEN US?"

SURE! I KNOW ALL ABOUT SANDING AND FINISHING WOOD NOW.

ONLY PROBLEM IS, THE FIREPLACE IS CAST IRON AND IT'S A BIT RUSTY. AND SOMEONE'S TRIED TO PAINT OVER THE TOP OF THE RUST. BUT I'M SURE THE OLD MAN AT THE DIY SHOP WILL BE ABLE TO TELL YOU WHAT TO DO. I'LL MEET YOU AT MY PLACE LATER.

FLASH
Is Kevin about to get out of his depth again? Read on...

HEAVY METAL
AND TOXIC CHEMICALS

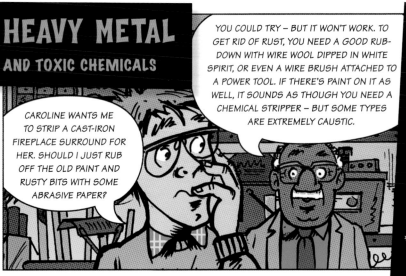

CAROLINE WANTS ME TO STRIP A CAST-IRON FIREPLACE SURROUND FOR HER. SHOULD I JUST RUB OFF THE OLD PAINT AND RUSTY BITS WITH SOME ABRASIVE PAPER?

YOU COULD TRY – BUT IT WON'T WORK. TO GET RID OF RUST, YOU NEED A GOOD RUB-DOWN WITH WIRE WOOL DIPPED IN WHITE SPIRIT, OR EVEN A WIRE BRUSH ATTACHED TO A POWER TOOL. IF THERE'S PAINT ON IT AS WELL, IT SOUNDS AS THOUGH YOU NEED A CHEMICAL STRIPPER – BUT SOME TYPES ARE EXTREMELY CAUSTIC.

CAPTAIN'S KIT
* heavy-duty protective gloves
* safety goggles and mask
* chemical stripper
* old paintbrush
* wire wool * white spirit
* rust inhibitor
* black lead or aerosol paint
* metal primer, if necessary
* soft, clean cloths
* hammer and chisel
* screwdriver
* chimney-sweeping brush
* dust sheets * brush and shovel
* drill and bit
* long plugs and screws

I'VE REMOVED PAINT WITH STRIPPERS BEFORE [SEE PAGE 140]. WHAT SHOULD I PUT ON WHEN IT'S STRIPPED BACK TO BARE METAL?

I RECOMMEND A RUST INHIBITOR. THERE'S ONE HERE THAT'S GOT A BUILT-IN PRIMER. OTHERWISE, YOU'D HAVE TO APPLY A SEPARATE ZINC PHOSPHATE PRIMER BEFORE YOU COULD APPLY A FINISH ON TOP.

NOW, FOR THE FINISH, MY PERSONAL FAVOURITE ON CAST IRON IS BLACK LEAD. ALTERNATIVELY, IF YOU WANT TO PAINT IT ANOTHER COLOUR, USE AN AEROSOL PAINT TO GET INTO ALL THE INTRICATE MOULDINGS. OF COURSE, YOU'LL HAVE TO WORK IN A WELL-VENTILATED AREA AND MASK OFF SURROUNDING AREAS. THESE ARE PRETTY SCARY CHEMICALS TO USE, KEVIN.

BEFORE YOU START, MAKE SURE THAT THE FIREPLACE REALLY IS CAST IRON. SOME FIREPLACE SURROUNDS ARE JUST PLASTER ON A WOODEN SURROUND. TAP IT AND LISTEN, OR SCRATCH A BIT AWAY TO MAKE SURE. AND MY NAME IS DAVID, NOT 'OLD MAN'.

DON'T WORRY ABOUT ME, OLD MAN. ONE THING I'VE LEARNED RECENTLY IS ALWAYS TO READ THE INSTRUCTIONS.

ISN'T IT GREAT? I MEASURED AND IT'S EXACTLY THE RIGHT SIZE TO REPLACE THE OLD FIREPLACE SURROUND IN MY SITTING ROOM.

YOU'RE GOING TO HAVE TO STAND WELL BACK, CAROLINE. SEEMINGLY THIS STRIPPER COULD EVEN MELT MY SPECTACLES IF I SPLASHED ANY ON THEM.

1 Apply the stripper, leave it on for the recommended time, then scrape off as much of the resulting goo as you can. Scrub it with wire wool dipped in stripper to get any last specks of paint off. Neutralize it with either water or white spirit, depending on the manufacturer's instructions.

2 Use an old paintbrush to apply the rust inhibitor, working it in well.

THIS STUFF GIVES THE IRON A PROTECTIVE COATING SO AIR AND WATER CAN'T GET TO IT AND CAUSE RUST. THE CAPTAIN WOULD BE VERY PROUD IF HE COULD SEE ME NOW.

UGH! DON'T MENTION THAT SNARKY SUPERHERO TO ME!

THE DESIGN IS SO ORNATE THAT I CAN'T REACH INTO THE DEEPEST BITS. DO YOU HAVE AN OLD TOOTHBRUSH I COULD USE?'

3 After the rust inhibitor has done its work, Kevin wipes it down with white spirit. Caroline agrees that the black lead finish will look nice, so he applies it with a soft cloth, rubbing it into all the crevices.

4 Buff the black lead to a sheen with a clean cloth. You may want to apply a few more coats for an attractive, moisture-resistant finish. Keep any black lead that you don't use, because the finish might need to be touched up in future.

WOW! IT LOOKS LIKE A MILLION DOLLARS!

FLASH
Eagle-eyed readers will have spotted the problem they're about to confront...

5 The Captain has to chip away the plaster all around the fireplace to find the fixing screws. They're old and rusty, so he has to prise them out with a crowbar before he can pull away the wooden fireplace surround.

6 The Captain decides to sweep the chimney while he's in the vicinity. If you fancy doing this yourself, be warned that it can make an unholy mess. Cover everything with dust sheets, including the fireplace, and get yourself a handy extendable chimney-sweeping brush.

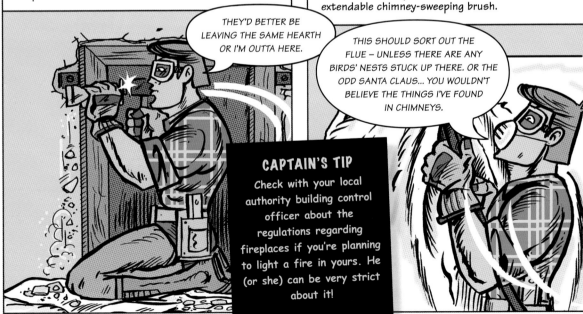

CAPTAIN'S TIP
Check with your local authority building control officer about the regulations regarding fireplaces if you're planning to light a fire in yours. He (or she) can be very strict about it!

7 Keep adding more extensions to the brush handle until it meets no resistance and you know you've reached the top. Move the brush up and down rather than screwing it around. When you've finished, shovel all the dirt into bin bags.

DON'T PUSH TOO HARD NEAR THE END, OR YOU COULD KNOCK YOUR CHIMNEY POT OFF.

TELL YOUR BOYFRIEND TO BE A BIT MORE REALISTIC IN FUTURE. NEVER START A DIY JOB UNTIL YOU'VE THOUGHT THROUGH EVERY ASPECT OF IT, INCLUDING PLANNING HOW YOU'RE GOING TO DEAL WITH HEAVY WEIGHTS.

LET'S GET THIS FIREPLACE IN POSITION. OH CRIPES, HEAVING HERNIAS! I THINK MY EYES ARE GOING TO POP OUT.

8 With great relief, the Captain rests the cast-iron surround in the fireplace and marks its fixing positions on the wall.

OF COURSE I'M ALL RIGHT. I COULD LIFT 20 OF THESE BABIES WITH ONE HAND. WHO DO YOU THINK YOU'RE TALKING TO?

IT WAS MY FAULT. SORRY, CAPTAIN – IT WON'T HAPPEN AGAIN.

OF COURSE, IF IT'S FOR YOU, I WOULD DO ANYTHING. ANYTHING AT ALL.

THANKS ANYWAY, BUT I'M SURE I WON'T BE NEEDING YOUR... ERM... SERVICES.

9 The Captain has to lift the fireplace away from the wall again to drill fixing holes and insert wallplugs, then he puts it back and screws it into position. He replasters the surrounding wall, but Kevin and Caroline will have to wait for the plaster to dry before they can redecorate on top of it.

GETTING IT OFF YOUR CHEST
STRIPPING WOODEN FURNITURE

DO YOU THINK WE CAN RENOVATE THE TEA-CHEST AND TABLE WITHOUT ASKING THE CAPTAIN'S HELP?

SURE! I KNOW HOW TO SAND AND FINISH WOOD NOW. I'LL USE A STRIPPER TO TAKE THE PAINT OFF THE TABLE, WHILE YOU CAN SAND THE CHEST WITH ABRASIVE PAPER.

HELLO, I NEED TO TALK TO YOU ABOUT STRIPPERS, DAVID.

OH, REALLY??**!!

YES. WHAT WOULD YOU USE TO STRIP PAINT FROM AN OLD WOODEN TABLE WITH FANCY LEGS?

IF YOU WANT TO EXPOSE THE WOOD, I WOULDN'T USE A HOT-AIR GUN BECAUSE THEY CAN SCORCH IT. AND SANDERS REMOVE THE TOP LAYER. SOUNDS AS THOUGH YOU NEED A GEL OR PASTE STRIPPER, BECAUSE LIQUID STRIPPERS WOULD JUST RUN OFF THE TABLE LEGS.

Seems Kevin is getting a bit more of an idea of what he's talking about.

I'LL TAKE THE PASTE STRIPPER, AND SOME POLYURETHANE VARNISH TO FINISH IT OFF. PLUS A WOOD STAIN FOR THE CHEST.

1 Kevin applies paste stripper all over the table. It can even be applied to the underside and it slips easily into the intricate carvings on the legs. The only downside with strippers is that they can slightly darken the wood – and once again they're very toxic chemicals, so cover up.

2 Caroline is sanding the chest while Kevin gives her instructions. Wrap your abrasive paper around a piece of dowel to reach into crevices.

ALWAYS SAND IN THE DIRECTION OF THE WOOD GRAIN. START WITH A COARSE PAPER, THEN MOVE TO MEDIUM. BEFORE THE FINAL SANDING, DAMPEN THE WOOD TO RAISE THE GRAIN AND LET IT DRY AGAIN, THEN FINISH OFF WITH THE FINEST GRADE OF PAPER.

3 Kevin's chemical stripper has worked now, so he scrapes the old paint off the table and neutralizes it according to the manufacturer's instructions (which he's actually read). Then he has to follow his own advice as he sands it.

COARSE TO MEDIUM TO FINE. OF _COARSE_ I KNOW WHAT I'M TALKING ABOUT. HA, HA.

IT WAS FUN STRIPPING WITH YOU. WHAT SHALL WE DO NEXT, KEVIN?

UM, WELL, ACTUALLY I PROMISED I'D GO TO MY MOTHER'S FOR DINNER. I'LL CATCH UP WITH YOU TOMORROW AND WE CAN PLAN OUR NEXT JOINT ACTIVITIES...

4 Kevin uses a clean paintbrush to apply a thin layer of matt varnish all over the table. This will give it a rich, hard-wearing finish. He'll need two or three coats, and it will be easier to apply if he thins the first coat with a small amount of white spirit.

VARNISH IS ANOTHER ULTRA-FLAMMABLE SUBSTANCE, SO NO PLAYING WITH MATCHES OUT HERE!

5 Caroline applies a nice beech wood stain to even out any last areas of discoloration on the chest, then she uses wax polish and some elbow grease to give a nice shiny finish (although it won't be as hard-wearing as varnish).

FLASH
Mmmm, saucy! Could DIY be bringing them closer together?

FRESH AND WARM
CREATING THE RIGHT ATMOSPHERE

CAPTAIN'S KIT
- blanket or loose-fill loft insulation
- wooden batten * scissors
- self-adhesive window and door draught excluders
- window vent or window extraction fan

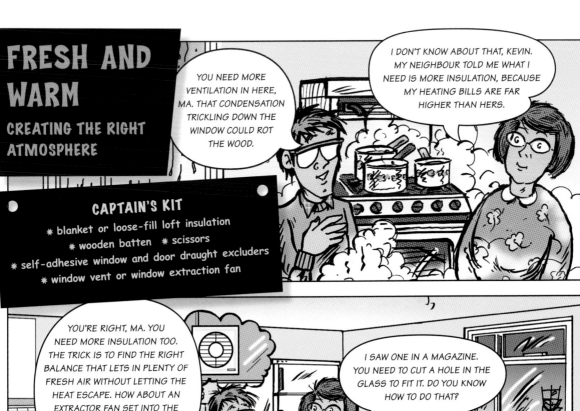

YOU NEED MORE VENTILATION IN HERE, MA. THAT CONDENSATION TRICKLING DOWN THE WINDOW COULD ROT THE WOOD.

I DON'T KNOW ABOUT THAT, KEVIN. MY NEIGHBOUR TOLD ME WHAT I NEED IS MORE INSULATION, BECAUSE MY HEATING BILLS ARE FAR HIGHER THAN HERS.

YOU'RE RIGHT, MA. YOU NEED MORE INSULATION TOO. THE TRICK IS TO FIND THE RIGHT BALANCE THAT LETS IN PLENTY OF FRESH AIR WITHOUT LETTING THE HEAT ESCAPE. HOW ABOUT AN EXTRACTOR FAN SET INTO THE WINDOW? IT COULD RELEASE COOKING SMELLS AS WELL AS WATER VAPOUR.

I SAW ONE IN A MAGAZINE. YOU NEED TO CUT A HOLE IN THE GLASS TO FIT IT. DO YOU KNOW HOW TO DO THAT?

I WOULDN'T DREAM OF CUTTING THROUGH GLASS MYSELF, BUT I COULD GET A GLAZIER TO SUPPLY A NEW PANE WITH A HOLE ALREADY CUT IN IT. OF COURSE, WE'D ALSO NEED AN ELECTRICIAN TO CONNECT IT TO THE MAINS – UNLESS I JUST BUY ONE OF THOSE SIMPLE VENTS THAT YOU CAN OPEN AND CLOSE BY HAND. BUT THEY'RE NOT VERY EFFECTIVE.

I'VE LEARNED MY LESSON ABOUT NOT DABBLING IN DANGEROUS AREAS, LIKE ELECTRICAL WIRING OR CUTTING THROUGH GLASS. BUT WHEN IT COMES TO SAVING ON YOUR HEATING BILLS, I KNOW JUST WHAT TO DO. REMEMBER LAST TIME IT SNOWED, AND THE SNOW ON YOUR ROOF MELTED ALMOST IMMEDIATELY WHILE IT STAYED WHITE AND CRISP ON YOUR NEIGHBOUR'S ROOF?

YOU'VE CHANGED RECENTLY, SON. YOU USED TO BE WILLING TO GIVE ANYTHING A TRY. HAVE YOU LOST YOUR NERVE?

ISN'T THAT A GOOD THING? IT MEANS MY HOUS IS WARMER THAN HERS.

WELL, NOW, ISN'T THAT CLEVER?

NO, IT MEANS YOUR ROOF IS WARMER THAN HERS, AND WHAT'S THE POINT IN HEATING A ROOF? TO KEEP THE BIRDS WARM? IF WE INSULATE YOUR LOFT FLOOR WITH BLANKET INSULATION, THE HEAT WILL BE TRAPPED IN THE HOUSE BELOW. IT'S EASY TO LAY – YOU JUST ROLL IT OUT BETWEEN THE JOISTS. IT DOESN'T NEED TO BE NAILED DOWN.

CAPTAIN'S TIP
Another way of insulating your loft floor is with loose-fill insulation. Simply tip out bags of it into the spaces between the joists and level it with a straightedge or a wooden batten.

WE'LL BUY A SPECIAL JACKET FOR YOUR HOT WATER CYLINDER AND STRAP IT ON. I MIGHT WRAP FOAM INSULATION AROUND SOME OF YOUR PIPEWORK AS WELL, SO YOU DON'T GET FROZEN PIPES IN WINTER.

AND SOME OF YOUR WINDOWS ARE A BIT DRAUGHTY. WE'LL STICK SOME SELF-ADHESIVE DRAUGHTPROOFING TAPE AROUND THE WINDOW FRAMES. THAT SHOULD CUT DOWN YOUR HEATING BILLS DRASTICALLY.

HOW DO YOU KNOW ALL THIS, KEVIN? DID YOU READ IT IN A BOOK?

NO, I'VE MADE THESE GREAT NEW FRIENDS, MA. ONE IS CALLED DAVID AND HE WORKS IN THE DIY STORE. THE OTHER'S CALLED THE CAPTAIN – AND HE JUST SEEMS TO APPEAR WHENEVER I NEED HIM.

THEY SOUND NICE. WHY DON'T YOU INVITE THEM AROUND FOR DINNER ONE NIGHT SO I CAN MEET THEM? BRING CAROLINE AS WELL.

HMM, NICE OFFER, BUT THAT WOULDN'T WORK. CAROLINE AND THE CAPTAIN DON'T EXACTLY SEE EYE TO EYE. HE THINKS HE'S A BIT OF A SUPERHERO TYPE, AND SHE JUST THINKS HE'S FULL OF HIMSELF.

DON'T YOU GO UPSETTING THAT NICE GIRL, KEVIN. IF SHE DOESN'T LIKE THE CAPTAIN, I'M SURE SHE'S GOT VERY GOOD REASONS.

FLASH
Does Caroline really dislike the Captain as much as Kevin thinks? Read on...

215

WORKING WITH THE PROS

OOH, I DON'T LIKE THE LOOK OF THIS. IT'S GOING TO COST YOU, GUV. HALF UP FRONT, THE REST TOMORROW, CASH ONLY, THAT'S THE DEAL.

As Kevin has learned, if you take on a DIY task that is beyond your capabilities, it can make a whole heap of mess! It's way more expensive bringing someone in to fix the damage afterwards than it would have been to hire a professional who knew what they were talking about in the first place. And – worst-case scenario – you risk serious injury if you don't accept your own limitations. There's no need to freak out when it's time to hire a pro; just follow our hot tips to ensure a problem-free experience...

BIG JOBS

If you're adding rooms, or changing the layout of existing ones, it's well worth hiring an architect. They'll point out any design glitches you might have overlooked, arrange permission from the local authorities and oversee work from start to finish to make sure it's up to scratch. Would you be able to spot if a builder was using sub-standard bricks? No, me neither – but your architect would.

For less drastic structural alterations, such as knocking down or building a wall, a good builder will oversee the work of any other professionals required: plasterers, plumbers, electricians, carpenters or gas installers. Watch out if they all seem to be his cousins, though.

FINDING THE GOOD GUYS

Personal recommendations are best. If they've done a good job for a friend, chances are they will for you too. Failing this, ask for references from previous clients and call to check them out. (Ask for a few, so it's not just their sister-in-law you talk to.) Check if they're affiliated to the relevant trade associations and make sure they have adequate insurance just in case they cause any damage in your home. Sorry to be so negative, but there are cowboys out there on the prairie.

CAPTAIN'S TIP: Contact your home insurance company to inform them of any major work and check that they will cover you while it's going on.

ESTIMATES AND CONTRACTS

Make sure all stages of the job are listed. If you simply ask a builder to knock a hole in a wall, a hole in the wall is what you'll get. Don't expect him to make good for decorating unless it's specified in the contract.

Ask for all materials to be noted, and check whether they're good-quality or cheap substitutes. (If you're friendly with the staff in your local builders' merchant, they should be able to glance

WHEN IT'S LIKE NIAGARA FALLS IN YOUR KITCHEN, TIME TO CALL IN THE PROFESSIONALS.

IF YOU HAVE A SUPERHERO OF YOUR OWN, MAKE SURE YOU CHERISH HIM. WE'RE LOYAL, PROTECTIVE AND CUDDLY.

at an estimate and give you an idea.) Some estimates list provisional sums, but you're within your rights to specify that your approval is sought before your money is spent.

Always insist on a contract, even if it's just a clearly written letter on headed notepaper. Check that all aspects of the job are described and schedules for completion are given. With small jobs where materials don't have to be purchased up front, the professional will probably accept payment on completion. For larger jobs, there may be interim payments linked to specific stages. With major building work, it's customary to hold back 10 per cent of the fee till six months after completion so you have time to check that plaster isn't cracking and ceilings haven't fallen down.

HELP YOUR PROS

Don't expect them to work around your household clutter. Clear carpets, furniture, laundry piles, children and pets well out of the way. If a job takes more than a day, it's wise to create a space where they can leave their tools overnight – that way, you know they're bound to come back!

And one last tip from the Captain: it's only polite to offer frequent refreshments to people working in your home. Two sugars in mine, please.

SAVING THE PLANET

GO GREEN WITH THE CAPTAIN

DON'T YOU JUST LOVE THE BIRDS AND THE BEES?

All superheroes have a mission – to rid the world of evil, rescue human beings from nasty accidents and save the planet from devastating disaster. Captain Competent feels especially strongly about conserving the Earth's natural resources – water, land, forests and fresh air – to prevent the destruction of life as we know it. Here are some tips on how you can help him in his quest.

WHAT A LOAD OF RUBBISH!

We're running out of landfill sites in the West, and incinerators produce toxic stuff called dioxins, which are linked with all sorts of health scares, so it's imperative that we become more responsible about our rubbish. Here's what you can do:

* Use your local authority recycling schemes. They will probably collect glass, paper and cans; some collect textiles as well. If there aren't any local schemes, lobby the authority to start some!
* Organic matter (food waste) produces methane gas when it breaks down, which contributes to pollution. If you collect yours in a composting bin, you can use it to fertilise the garden while protecting the atmosphere at the same time.
* Glass and plastics don't break down easily. Try to avoid buying overpackaged items, and use paper rather than plastic bags when shopping.

DON'T WASTE WATER

Even if you don't live in an area where there are water shortages, consider the energy it takes to bring fresh water to your taps and conserve it as much as you can:

* Fix leaks and dripping taps immediately (see pages 88–93).
* Shower rather than bathe. A three-minute shower uses just 41 litres (9 gallons) of water (power showers use rather more), compared to the 164 litres (36 gallons) in an average bath.
* Consider installing a water-saving device in your toilet. Let's face it – without getting too technical – we don't always need a full flush!
* Don't leave taps running while you brush your teeth or rinse dishes.
* Only run washing machines and dishwashers when you have a full load. This saves energy as well, bringing us on to the next point...

STOP GLOBAL WARMING

Carbon dioxide emissions from fuel consumption are a major contributor to the greenhouse effect, which is causing climate change and affecting the natural ecology of the planet. The North and South Poles are already melting, which is bad news for everyone, not just polar bears and penguins.

There are several ways to cut down your fuel use:

* Make sure your home is well-insulated. If heat is being lost through windows, walls, doors or roof, you are using more energy than you need to keep the temperature constant. Walk around the house on a windy day and see where draughts are coming in, and which parts feel coolest. Cavity-wall insulation and double glazing may be expensive, but they will eventually cover their costs in fuel bill savings (see pages 212–13 for some easier methods of insulating your home).
* Buy energy-efficient household appliances and light bulbs. They'll save you money all round.
* More and more people are using solar panels on their roofs to provide hot water and even heating. Why not look into it? Sunshine is free!

BE ECO-FRIENDLY

* Cleaning products contain all sorts of chemical nasties that enter the atmosphere and pollute waterways. Try to avoid products that contain chlorine (i.e. bleach) and phosphates. Choose safer alternatives.
* Paints, varnishes and paint removers can contain volatile organic compounds (VOCs), which contribute to air pollution and climate change – and the fumes can also make you feel very ill. Avoid vinyl resins and petrochemical solvents,

and opt for eco-friendly alternatives – there are loads available. You might need to scrub a bit harder without eye-watering chemical strippers, but think of the benefits for your biceps.
* Always consult your local authority for advice on disposing of any chemicals. Don't just pour them down the drain, or they'll turn up in your fish supper one day.

BE NICE TO TREES

* Never buy wood that doesn't come from a renewable resource. Don't just think about this when you're buying from a timber yard (see page 126) – ask in the furniture store where the wood for your new table came from. Look out for the FSC (Forest Stewardship Council) logo if you want to be a good global citizen.
* Buy recycled paper – it's every bit as good as non-recycled, and soft enough for use in the loo. You'll feel the warm glow of knowing the trees love you in return.

THE CAPTAIN'S JARGON
KNOW YOUR DIY LINGO!

ARCHITRAVE
The decorative bits of moulding around doors and windows.

BALLVALVE
The floating ball attached to an arm with a valve on the other end that you find in toilet cisterns. What did you think?

BEADING
A painting technique that is used to get a neat line where two colours meet.

CASEMENT WINDOW
The type of window that opens into and out of the room. See also sash windows.

CISTERN
A tank for storing water, usually in the roof space or connected to your loo to hold the water you will need when you want to flush (qv).

CONSUMER UNIT
Your main electricity circuit board, with a master on/off switch.

COUNTERSINK
To drive in a screw so that the top of the screw head is flush (qv) with the surface of the wood, rather than protruding above it.

CUTTING IN
Using a small brush or paint pad to blend in edges.

DEPTH STOP
A plastic guide or piece of tape stuck to a drill bit so you can see when you have drilled to the correct depth.

DOWEL
Wooden rods; they can be tiny, for filling screw holes, or large enough to hang curtains on.

FLUSH
1. Level with another surface.
2. To cause water to flood from a cistern into a toilet bowl, cleaning out the contents.

FUSE
A device containing a special kind of wire that will melt if an electric circuit is overloaded, cutting off the flow of electricity. Can also be used as a verb, i.e. the lights fused. See also MCB and RCD.

GRIPPERS
Metal strips with rows of little spikes for fixing carpets to floors.

GROMMETS
Rings of rubber or plastic that are used to line holes to stop any cables that run through them from chafing and wearing out.

GROUT
Waterproof filler used to seal joints between tiles.

JUMPERS
Fiddly little bits inside taps.

MINIATURE CIRCUIT BREAKER (MCB)
Like a fuse (qv) this breaks an electrical circuit in the event of a fault, but it does so by means of a trip switch that can be reset when the fault has been repaired.

MORTISE LOCK
A mortise lock is recessed in the edge of a door. It contains a steel bolt that shoots out when the key is turned. When the bolt fits into a keeper in your door frame, the door is locked.

PILE
The tufty bits that stick up from the backing of a carpet.

PRIMER
A first coat applied to wood, metal or plaster so that subsequent coats of paint will adhere nicely.

REBATES
Grooves that panes of glass fit into around the edge of a window frame.

RESIDUAL CURRENT DEVICE (RCD)
A trip switch that cuts off the flow of electricity if you do something silly, like cutting through or drilling into an electric cable.

RISERS
The vertical bits of your stairs. The horizontal bits are called treads.

SASH WINDOW
Opens by sliding panels (sashes) up and down – or, sometimes, from side to side.

SPACERS
Little plastic things used for maintaining even spaces between tiles for grout (qv) to be applied, or between flooring strips and walls to allow for expansion.

STOPTAP
A valve that stops liquid flowing along a pipe.

STRIPPERS
Use these to remove paint, varnish, wallpaper or any other undesirable coating from a surface.

STUD
A wooden vertical inside a cavity or partition wall. Stud walls can consist of plasterboard nailed to a wooden framework, or horizontal laths nailed between studs.

THREAD
The spiral grooves on the flank of a screw.

TONGUE-AND-GROOVE
A type of floor (or wall) board where a tongue slots into a groove on the previous board, thus holding them together.

FURTHER READING

100 THINGS YOU DON'T NEED A MAN FOR
Alison Jenkins
(Aurum Press, 2001)

1001 DIY HINTS AND TIPS
(Reader's Digest, 1999)

COLLINS COMPLETE DIY MANUAL
Albert Jackson and David Day
(Collins, 2001)

COLLINS COMPLETE PLUMBING AND CENTRAL HEATING
Albert Jackson and David Day
(Collins, 2004)

COMPLETE BOOK OF DIY, DECORATION AND HOME IMPROVEMENT
Mike Lawrence
(Southwater, 2004)

THE COMPLETE GUIDE TO WALLPAPERING
David M. Groff (Creative Homeowner Press, 1999)

HANDY ANDY'S HOME WORK: A BEGINNER'S GUIDE TO DECORATING, DIY, AND MAINTENANCE
Andy Kane
(BBC Consumer Publishing, 2000)

INSTALLING & FINISHING FLOORING
William P Spence
(Sterling, 2003)

THE NEW COMPLETE BOOK OF DECORATIVE PAINT TECHNIQUES
Anne Sloan and Kate Gwynn (Ebury Press, 1999)

THE PRACTICAL BOOK OF HOME DIY
Mike Lawrence
(Southwater, 2001)

READER'S DIGEST COMPLETE DIY MANUAL
(Reader's Digest, 2003)

THE WALL TILING BOOK
Alex Portelli
(Haynes Publishing, 1995)

WHICH? BOOK OF DIY
Mike Lawrence
(Which? Books, 1999)

YOU CAN DO IT: THE COMPLETE B&Q STEP-BY-STEP BOOK OF HOME IMPROVEMENT
Nicholas Barnard (Editor), (Thames & Hudson, 2003)

USEFUL CONTACTS

PAINTS AND FINISHES
CROWN PAINTS
Tel: 0870 240 1127
www.crownpaints.co.uk

DULUX
Tel: 01753 550 555
www.dulux.co.uk

HAMMERITE
Tel: 01661 830000
www.hammerite.co.uk

RONSEAL
Tel: 0114 2467171
www.ronseal.co.uk

FLOORING
ALLIED CARPETS
Tel: 08000 932932
www.alliedcarpets.co.uk

AMTICO
Tel: 08000 932932
www.amtico.co.uk

CRUCIAL TRADING
Tel: 01562 743 747
www.crucial-trading.com

PERGO
Tel: 0800 374771
www.pergo.com

WALLCOVERINGS
COLOROLL
Tel: 01282 727400
www.coloroll.co.uk

GRAHAM & BROWN
Tel: 0800 868100
www.grahambrown.com

TILES
FIRED EARTH
Tel: 01295 814315
www.firedearth.co.uk

JUST TILES
Tel: 0118 969 7774
www.justtiles.co.uk

DIY SUPERSTORES
B&Q
Tel: 0845 309 3099
www.diy.com

FOCUS
Tel: 0800 436 436
www.focusdiy.co.uk

HOMEBASE
Tel: 0845 077 8888
www.homebase.co.uk

WICKES
Tel: 0870 6089001
www.wickes.co.uk

OTHER USEFUL WEBSITES
DIY DOCTOR
www.diydoctor.org.uk

DIY FIXIT
www.diyfixit.co.uk

NO, YOU CAN'T HAVE MY PHONE NUMBER!

iNDEX

ACKNOWLEDGEMENTS

Grateful thanks to Professor John Paul for some hints, tips and shortcuts learned during his 50-plus years' experience of fixing things that break around the home.

Huge thanks to Caroline Earle for being such a Superhero Editor – and for letting us base Kevin's girlfriend on her!

In loving memory of Bette Paul – wife, mother, grandmother, best friend and party girl extraordinaire.

PLEASE DON'T LEAVE ME, CAPTAIN.

YOU'LL HAVE MY BOOK FOR ADVICE!